THE WESTERN OCEAN PASSENGER LINES AND LINERS

A

BY THE SAME AUTHOR

Passenger Liners of the Westers Ocean

First Edition, 1952

Second (and Enlarged) Edition, 1957

British Passenger Liners of the Five Oceans

QUEEN MARY

THE OLD RIVALS

NORMANDIE

Frontispiece

THE WESTERN OCEAN PASSENGER LINES AND LINERS

1934-1969

Commander C. R. Vernon Gibbs,
Royal Navy

GLASGOW
BROWN, SON & FERGUSON, LTD.
52 Darnley Street

First Printed - 1970

Printed and Made in Great Britain

'We twa hae paddl'd in the burn
'Frae morning sun till dine,
'But seas between us braid hae roar'd
'Sin auld lang syne.'

This Book on the Mid-20th Century North Atlantic Liners is dedicated to the Memory of the Common Folk who endured a Steerage Crossing of the Western Ocean last Century and never returned to the British Shores.

LIST OF CONTENTS

(* Indicates that the Line is still operating a transatlantic passenger service. Several former transatlantic lines remain in business, however, though now confined to pleasure-cruising.)

LIST OF ILLUSTRATIONS

PREFACE AND ACKNOWLEDGMENTS

THE Western Ocean is, of course, the North Atlantic and seafaring men rarely use any other name when talking among themselves. Although the narrowest of the oceans, it is alike the most boisterous and most important. None has carried a greater volume of trade; none so great a number of ships and until the very recent advent of mammoth tankers the Western Ocean's giant ships have dwarfed all others.

Earliest recorded crossing of the Western Ocean from Europe took place only five years after Columbus had penetrated into the sub-tropical Central Atlantic and gained the West Indies. In May 1497, John Cabot's *Mathew*, manned with a crew of 18, dropped down the Avon on the ebb, almost within sight of where this book is written, and reached Nova Scotia in 52 days. Bristol became England's ocean-gateway to the West, as London to the Eastern Seas. Pride of place passed to Liverpool during the 18th Century, but this did not prevent Cabot's city ushering in the era of Western Ocean steam navigation. The first Atlantic steamship (*Great Western*) and the pioneer iron-hulled deep-sea screw vessel (*Great Britain*) both took shape on the left bank of the Avon, and it was from here that the former began her epic Atlantic voyage, April 1838. Bristol was to see her last passenger sailing for New York a mere four years later, but *Great Western* and *Great Britain* were the progenitors of every liner which followed in their wakes. Pleasure-cruising has become popular, but the passenger liner is now passing as a simple transport medium and the newest (*Queen Elizabeth* 2) publicised as providing 'a holiday in itself' rather than a surface means of transatlantic travel. This book is devoted to what appear to be the closing years of the true Western Ocean passenger liner.

My object has been to describe the present ships and those which remain 'living memories' for men and women not yet in retirement. The year, 1934, almost chooses itself as my starting-point. By then the World Depression, which began five years before, had reduced the number of North Atlantic passenger lines and shortened the fleet-lists of most of the survivors. Many liners built before the 1914–18 War were still gainfully employed during the 1920's, but by 1934 the shipbreaker had claimed practically all. The World Depression of the early 1930's created a more real break in the continuity of Western Ocean shipping history than either of the World Wars.

The Western Ocean Passenger Lines and Liners, 1934–1969, is complete in itself, but also supplements my *Passenger Liners of the Western Ocean*, of which the last text was written 13 years ago. These years have witnessed many changes, including the inauguration (and sometimes, closure) of new passenger services across the North Atlantic, but perhaps the withering away of the Canadian traffic has been the most pronounced. Differentiation between the New York and the St. Lawrence trades in the book's arrangement has become pointless. Where ships' particulars, etc., given in this present work disagree with those in my earlier books, I should like the newer text accepted, bearing in mind that the older texts give 'as built' figures for pre-1934 vessels and the present 'as in 1934'. I wish, moreover, to take this opportunity to correct a most unfortunate mistake appearing on page 38 of *Passenger Liners of the Western Ocean* (Second Edition). Feathering paddles were never used on the North Atlantic except by *Connaught* of the short-lived Galway Line. All other paddles were fixed, although different types tried.

I have endeavoured to make the illustrations fully representative and choice has often been guided by the desire to show the funnel of a particular company. Many readers will notice that I have omitted the customary definite article before the names of ships. The omission has been made deliberately in the belief that it lightens the reading of a book so heavily weighted with ship-names and I can only hope that readers will agree.

My most grateful acknowledgments are due to the very many bodies and individuals who have helped in producing the text and illustrations of *The Western Ocean Passenger Lines and Liners, 1934–1969*. The extant transatlantic passenger shipping companies have all been lavish with their assistance, and the help received from the Steamship Historical Society of America cannot be rated too highly. The columns of *Sea Breezes* have made substantial contributions, and I must forget neither the Bristol City Central Library nor Lloyd's Register of Shipping. Turning to individual helpmates, I will begin on the other side of the Western Ocean by naming Mr. C. Bradford Mitchell, Mr. Frank O. Braynard and Mr. Wm. B. Saphire of New York, together with Mr. R. W. Parkinson of Berkeley (California) and Miss Annette Wolff of Montreal. To Dr. Arnold Rehm of Bremen and Dr. F. de Rossi of Naples, I am greatly indebted for information about the German and Italian companies. At home much help has come from Mr. J. H. Isherwood of Southampton and Mr. J. G. Wallace (formerly White Star Line) and Mr. A. L. Birrs (formerly Canadian Pacific Line) of Edinburgh. I must thank Mr. R. W. Lawes of the Port of Bristol Authority for the house-flag drawings and Mrs. E. Culton of Portishead for typing and much monotonous checking. Finally, I wish to express my feeling of indebtedness to the publishers, Brown, Son & Ferguson, Ltd., who have conceded everything I asked of them. My list of acknowledgments would still be incomplete if I failed to mention the late Mr. Frank C. Bowen without whose kindly tutelage in past years this book would never have been written.

Bristol, 1969 C.R.V.G.

PUBLISHERS NOTE

Shortly after work had commenced the author died suddenly. The Publishers have endeavoured to comply with his wishes, in the production on similar lines to his previous books, to make it uniform with them. Sincere thanks are due to the Author's widow for her assistance and advice. Also to Captain A. P. Atwill, C.B.E., R.N., for the proof reading and his helpful suggestions, which have assisted the Publishers in making possible the publication of the book. No correspondence could be found giving permission to use all the illustrations included. The Publishers are indebted to the shipping companies and others for the use of the photographs.

Explanatory Chapter

Scope of the Book. 'The Western Ocean Passenger Lines and Liners, 1934–69' is intended to cover the passenger lines and liners which have operated between Europe and the Eastern Mediterranean, and North American ports north of the Chesapeake over the last 36 years. 'Passenger Liner' of course means a ship licensed as such and has been confined to vessels in which passages have been freely bookable. Ocean cruising ships of the regular North Atlantic companies have also been included. Liners making transatlantic crossings as part of longer voyages have been excluded. Vessels launched for regular North Atlantic work but not employed as originally intended, are shown with their names enclosed in brackets.

Chapter and Sub-Chapter Headings. Dates indicate the years in which the company has operated transatlantic passenger ships (other than essentially emigrant-carriers). War has frequently brought complete suspension of sailings, but such breaks have been ignored except in the cases of the Norddeutscher Lloyd and the Hamburg-American Line where they have been lengthy. Nationality of the companies has been shown where necessary.

Funnels, House-Flags and Hull Colours. Information under these headings applies only to the passenger ships of 1934 and later years.

Funnel-tops are usually about one-quarter the depth of the whole funnel. Bands should be read downwards and immediately adjoin each other or any coloured funnel-top.

House-flag colours should be read from hoist to the fly or from top to bottom. A burgee is a swallow-tail flag.

In the absence of contrary information hulls should be presumed to be plain black and waterlines red. Ribands have been indicated, but it has not been possible to give white upper-strakes owing to their wide variations. Cruising-liners are often painted white, regardless of the usual company colours.

Arrangement, etc., of Ships. Ships have been arranged in the order of entry into service and, where applicable, in classes.

A liner's history has been presented as a continuous narrative despite any changes of owner and/or name, but an appropriate cross-reference made where alteration of ownership occurred.

The headings covering some less important vessels have been made in different style from the remainder.

An abbreviated date in brackets directly after a ship's name gives the date of completion where this differs from entry into the North Atlantic passenger trade.

An "(O)" signifies that a vessel was operated by the company under which shown, although not owned.

Dates of Employment. The dates following a ship's name represent those employed on the North Atlantic or cruising for a North Atlantic company, although there are some modifications. Where name/ownership has altered they are continuous unless the contrary is indicated.

The dates of former Atlantic liners which have been used for pleasure-cruising after the owning company dropped out of the transatlantic passenger trade have been kept open until sale.

The final year shown is usually that of sale or loss. Sale was to shipbreakers unless stated otherwise. Interruptions attributable to the two World Wars have been ignored. Where, however, a liner was requisitioned for war purposes and survived but did not return to her pre-war employment, the year of requisitioning appears as her final date.

Dates include any periods laid up in reserve or on charter to another company.

Ships have often been withdrawn from service and offered for sale late in the year, although actually sold a few weeks inside the next. In such instances the earlier year has been shown.

Where Built. With many shipyards the location of the yard is enough for identification purposes, but in other cases name of the builder has been added in abbreviated form. The abbreviated builder's name has been considered sufficient for most of the Clyde and Tyne yards.

Dimensions, General Particulars and Speed. These are 'as built' except for pre-1934 ships where they are given as in 1934 and sometimes differ substantially from the original. Items appear in the following order—

(*a*) *Gross Tonnage to the nearest 50 Tons.* (*See* below for measurements by United States', Panamanian and Liberian rules.)

(*b*) *Length-Between-Perpendiculars and Beam.* As an indication of relative capacity only length between perpendiculars is of value and the rules governing this measurement were changed in 1955 when length-overall replaced it as a ship's registered length. The old length-between-perpendiculars roughly corresponded with length of the upper-deck; the new (called 'moulded length' for some years) is length at the summer load-line and hence takes no account of the pronounced raked stems which have become so popular since the 1939–45 War. The length quoted is by the new rules wherever available and the old, where used, is set in italic type. Difference between the two would have been considerable in the cases of the record-breakers, but very small in other vessels.

(*c*) *Number of Funnels and Masts.* An asterisk indicates that one funnel, almost always the after one, was a dummy. Occasionally this dummy funnel served as exhaust for auxiliary machinery.

(*d*) *Type of Main Machinery and Number of Screws.* The following abbreviations are used for machinery-types—

3E, 4E or 3ET = Triple-Expansion, Quadruple-Expansion or Triple-Expansion with a Low-Pressure Turbine turning a separate screw.

T or GT – = Turbine (Direct Action) or Geared-Turbine.

M – – = Motor (Diesel).

TE – – = Turbo-Electric.

(*e*) *Speed.* A writer has no greater problem than ascribing to ships, speeds which are comparable with one another. There are many kinds of speed—maximum on trials, mean on trials, contract, service sea-speed, etc.—and unfortunately authorities who consistently quote the same kind of speed and/or specify which speed they are quoting are the exception. Speeds cited in *Lloyd's Register* are as supplied by owners and comparisons quickly bring out glaring anomalies. A further difficulty arises from the fact that outstandingly fast liners are designed to have an extra knot or so in reserve which is only used in emergency to recover time lost through weather, delays in port, etc. The figures given in this book represent estimated maximum speed throughout an Atlantic crossing under reasonably favourable weather conditions. Assessment is frequently a matter of judgment and allowance should be made for a possible error of a half-knot.

United States', Panamanian and Liberian Measurements. Gross tonnage measurements by the rules of the United States, Panama and Liberia are markedly lower than their European equivalents and worthless for comparative purposes. In most instances, however, measurements according to European standards are known and these have been substituted for the registered gross tonnage. Where necessary approximate tonnage by British rules has been estimated.

Fuel. Steamships are oil-fired except where otherwise stated.

Passenger Accommodation. Particulars of accommodation in 1934 of ships of earlier date are rarely available, although considerable alterations had usually been made. In particular, half or even more of the Third Class had been changed to Tourist in most Atlantic liners. Numbers carried are therefore shown 'as built' unless the contrary is indicated.

Designation of Classes. Basic standards in the majority of ships are much the same, but in the poorer vessels are apt to fall below the average and this has been implied where applicable.

A more serious difficulty arises from post-1945 misuse of the designation, 'Cabin Class'. The term was originally coined with the specific purpose of indicating that the Class concerned was the best in the ship. It began by covering a Second Class standard, although this steadily rose until it became closer to First in later vessels. The years 1936-39 were a confused period in which 'First' and 'Second' were actually merged and called 'Cabin'. (See *Queen Mary*, page 34.) Even then the term's fundamental meaning continued unchanged, since every Cabin Class passenger had access to the best decks and public rooms. After World War II the North Atlantic companies actually reversed the meaning by employing 'Cabin' to cover a Class which, although better than Tourist, denied passengers use of the most attractive parts of the ship. *Pre-war Cabin Class was the best a ship had to offer; post-war on the North Atlantic, a ship's second-grade accommodation.* A sharp difference between the two exists and *the post-war has therefore been described as 'Second Class' throughout this book.*

Third Class did not survive the 1939–45 World War, but a number of smaller vessels catering principally for migrants berthed all or part of their Tourist Class in 'dormitories' instead of cabins. Fares were low and such accommodation can be regarded as replacing the old Third. This 'dormitory' accommodation has been mentioned in the text where necessary.

North Atlantic Passenger Conference. The Conference consists of representatives of the North Atlantic passenger shipping companies. A main purpose is grading vessels according to the standard of accommodation, etc., provided and thence reaching agreement as to basic passage rates to be charged. Factors affecting basic fare in any particular liner are scheduled passage time and whether or not the Class concerned is the best in the ship. Hence, in 1934 one vessel's Cabin Class fare was higher than another's Second, although the only difference between the two ships was that one also carried First Class passengers. A result of this is that today's Western Ocean liners accommodating several hundred Tourist travellers always add a few First Class berths so that they may charge a lower and more competitive Tourist fare.

Cruising. Since the mid-1960's practically every Western Ocean passenger liner has done a little pleasure-cruising during the winter, even though not a dual-purpose ship.

Dual-purpose liners merge their passenger Classes into one when employed on cruises and the total numbers carried are reduced by about 25 per cent.

'Twelves'. Passenger vessels are built to higher specifications for stability, etc., than cargo ships, but the latter are permitted to carry passengers up to a maximum number of 12. Such cargo vessels are commonly referred to as 'Twelves'.

Record and Other Fast Passages. The real worth of a speedy ship is measured in regularity of performance, freedom from vibration, absence of technical troubles and economy of operation. Record-breaking by fractions of a knot made sensational headlines, but is best dismissed with a smile and the recollection that acceptance of the competitors' own figures for the mileage covered made this 'race' quite unique. Happily the days of Atlantic record-breaking belong to the past.

Voyage. The correct meaning of voyage is a double-passage, out and home, but the word is now popularly used to indicate a single passage. 'Round-voyage' has therefore been employed to cover a double-passage.

Halifax. During the 1950's and 1960's the less important liners bound for New York have frequently carried Canadian migrants and called at Halifax, but made no corresponding call on the eastward crossing.

CHAPTER I

British Line — The Cunard

CUNARD LINE (1840–)

FUNNEL – (a) *Red with black top and three black rings (the lowest ring usually concealed by the superstructure)*

(b) Queen Elizabeth 2 *only. White and dark grey* (see *illustration on page 81*)

FLAG – *The earlier Cunard flag* (see *below*) *flown over the former White Star (a red swallowtail-pennant bearing a 5-pointed white star). Cunard, red with gold badge*

HULL – Caronia *was painted three shades of green—a mid-green riband, a light green below and a still lighter green above—and* Mauretania, Carmania *and* Franconia *were similarly painted at the beginning of 1963. Four years later the hulls of* Carmania, Franconia *and* Sylvania *were changed to white*

Former White Star liners retained the White Star funnel (deep buff with black top) and hull (black with gold riband). They also flew the White Star pennant over the Cunard flag until 1951

With a solitary exception the North Atlantic steamship companies, founded before mid-19th century, proved ephemeral, many lasting no longer than three or four years. The exception was the British & North American Royal Mail Steam Packet Company, whose survival could largely be attributed to a generous, though reasonable, mail subsidy. The subsidy was almost halved in 1868 and 10 years afterwards efficient and increasing competition enabled the British Government to abolish the mail contract altogether. The 1870's saw the British & North American topple from the proud position so long occupied and the company's fortunes at a low ebb. Complete reconstruction, more money and fresh blood were needed. The undertaking became a public one at close of the decade. A new funnel and new house-flag were adopted, and a new name for the company was also desirable. The British & North American had begun as the brain-child of Samuel Cunard (died

1865) and here was a really distinctive name under which a brilliant resurrection could be staged—the Cunard Steam-Ship Company. If the new title had not incorporated 'Cunard', the generally accepted interpretation of the line's beginnings would probably have given more attention to Samuel Cunard's associates.

The idea of fortnightly steam sailings for North America (monthly in winter) certainly originated with Cunard himself, but the idea alone was far from enough. Co-signatories of the contract with the British Government were two firmly-established ship-owners already in partnership, George Burns and David MacIver. Indications leave little doubt that Burns and MacIver provided most of the British & North American Company's initial capital, although their proportion probably diminished later. Frequent, regular sailings plus the experience and money of Burns and MacIver, however, still remained insufficient to bring success. Many an early steamship company was to collapse within two or three years because the founders failed to appreciate the physical difficulties of their project, and this too would have been the fate of the British & North American without the technical foresight of a Clyde engineer, Robert Napier. Three steamers of around 600 tons had been contemplated; but Napier insisted that nothing less than four of double the size would suffice and the *Britannia*s measured 1150 tons. Napier was undoubtedly correct and major credit for the incipient Cunard Line's success seems rightfully to belong to him.

A generalised reference to the policy whereby the line's fortunes were restored nearly a century ago is perhaps permissible. Rival companies sought outstanding speeds; the Cunard aimed at speed-with-comfort, leaving others to experiment with over-engined hulls, twin-screws, etc. Preference for the proved, rather than the novel and sensational, continued over the years and can even be seen in *Queen Mary*, an orthodox and less-luxurious liner than the revolutionary *Normandie*, but so far as can be judged more profitable. Building of the record-smashing *Lusitania* and *Mauretania* in the early 1900's was forced on the Cunard by the pressure of events and represented the one break in this cautious policy.

During the 1920's *Mauretania*, *Aquitania* and the ex-German *Berengaria* gave the Cunard an express service between Southampton and New York which was certainly the finest of any company. War losses among the 'intermediate' steamers had been heavy and little time was wasted after conclusion of hostilities in ordering a dozen new ships for the New York and St. Lawrence trades from Liverpool and London (calling at Southampton). This enormous building programme enabled the Cunard Steam-Ship to maintain a multiplicity of passenger services between the World Wars which no other Western Ocean company could equal. The 1935–39 pattern differed little from the 1920's and was—

Express Mail—Southampton–Cherbourg–New York (weekly)
Intermediate— Liverpool–Cobh–New York (weekly)
London–Southampton–Havre–New York (fortnightly)
London–Southampton–Havre–Canada (weekly)
Liverpool–Greenock–Belfast–Canada (fortnightly)

Canadian voyages were either to Quebec and Montreal or to Halifax and New York, according to season. Of the 'intermediate' services the two weekly and the Liverpool–Canada were worked by ships of the immediate post-war programme. Unfortunately these had been designed in the belief, shared by all, that 16 knots would suffice for New York 'intermediates' and 15 for Canadian. The belief proved erroneous and soon rival companies were ordering faster vessels of this category. Cunard strength and weakness were brought home to the author in the 1920's when travelling in an 'intermediate' which had left New York a few minutes after midnight. The match-boxes in the public rooms bore the slogan, 'Travel Cunard always; Travel Cunard all ways', but during the first 36 hours three 'intermediates' belonging to other lines steamed past on a similar course for Europe.

The Express Service claimed attention when the Norddeutscher Lloyd *Bremen* ended *Mauretania*'s long reign as the swiftest Atlantic liner. Cunard reaction was to plan two enormous vessels able to maintain the existing weekly sailing schedule which required three. The first, *Queen Mary*, was laid down in December 1930, although the worst trade recession of modern times had set in a year earlier. The total number of transatlantic passengers carried by all the lines combined which had been 1,069,000 in 1929 was to fall to 685,000 in 1931 and touch bottom three years later with 460,000. The company found itself unable to continue financing construction of the new ship and work stopped. The recession which hit the Cunard had reduced the White Star Line to desperate straits. The Royal Mail Group had paid an excessive price in 1927 when restoring the White Star to British ownership by purchase from the International Mercantile Marine Company (*see* page 58). Construction of essential new ships (*Britannic* and *Georgic*) at Belfast had only been made feasible with money lent by the Northern Ireland Government and this prevented the British Government viewing collapse with equanimity. The latter therefore advanced £3 million to complete *Queen Mary* on condition that the Cunard and White Star lines amalgamated. *Queen Mary* went to sea in 1936 and recovered the coveted 'Blue Riband' for her owners, although the French *Normandie* [145] ran her very close indeed. A further government loan allowed work on her consort, *Queen Elizabeth*, to start the same year.

Fusion of Britain's two leading North Atlantic lines was attained by means of a holding-company, Cunard White Star Line Ltd., with effect from 1 January 1934. Use of the name, Cunard White Star Line, and the White Star vessels' retention of their old colours, hardly disguised the fact that the senior line had in effect absorbed the younger. Most of the White Star fleet was sold and only *Britannic* and *Georgic* left running at the end of 1936. The Cunard White Star era finished in 1947 when the Cunard Steam-Ship Company eliminated the White Star element by purchase and the holding company was wound up.

Many Cunarders became armed merchant cruisers at commencement of the 1939–45 War and all were trooping by the time it ended. A temporary cargo fleet took the place of the absent passenger liners, as in World War I. *Queen Elizabeth* cleared Southampton for New York, 25 October 1946, on the first Cunard post-war passenger sailing and the reconditioned *Queen Mary* joined her nine months later. *Ascania* re-established the Canadian service in December 1947, sailing from the Mersey, and the last Cunard steamer was de-requisitioned two years afterwards. Passenger construction over this period consisted of two small Liverpool–New York ships and *Caronia*, designed for long-distance cruising.

The year 1947 was a turning-point in Cunard history. The company has been a leading cargo-carrier as well as passenger for over a century and freight was the main revenue source in many ships. Nevertheless, it was not until 1947 that the Cunard began formation of a peacetime fleet of exclusively cargo liners with *Asia* and *Arabia*. In 1954–57 came the *Saxonia* quartette and these ships, too, marked a new departure. Size, speed and style of accommodation enabled them to win a share of the highest-grade Canadian passenger traffic.

The passenger fleet reached its post-1945 zenith with commissioning of the *Saxonia* and passenger services became—

Southampton – Cherbourg – New York (weekly by *Queen Elizabeth* and *Queen Mary*)
Southampton–Havre–Cobh–New York (by a new *Mauretania*)
Liverpool–Cobh–Havre (by *Britannic*)
Liverpool–New York direct (fortnightly by *Media* and *Parthia*)
Southampton–Havre–Cobh–Canada (two weeks out of three)
Liverpool–Greenock–Canada (two weeks out of three)

Canadian winter voyages were to Halifax, continuing to New York as in earlier years. *Caronia* cruised from New York throughout the year and also *Mauretania* and *Britannic* during the winter months.

Serious erosion of seaborne North Atlantic passenger traffic began during the 1950's and by 1957 the transatlantic airlines carried as many travellers—1 million—as the ships of all countries combined. The shipping companies' position worsened rapidly until eight years later they accounted for only 650,000 passengers, compared with the airlines' 4 million. Inevitably they began withdrawing passenger liners without replacement or using them increasingly for pleasure-cruising and the change was facilitated by the build-up of their freighter fleets. At the close of 1967 all the Cunard passenger services except the fast Southampton–Cherbourg–New York had ceased. A long and vital chapter in the North Atlantic story ended when Liverpool's last passenger liner, bound for New York, *Sylvania*, left the Mersey Bar Lightship astern, November 1966. Liverpool departures for Canada became once every three weeks in 1961 and after 1961–62 the Southampton Canadian service was suspended every winter. A 1968 programme showing regular Montreal voyages was published, but cancelled before the year began and what remained of the St. Lawrence passenger business was left to the Canadian Pacific.

The planning of a replacement for *Queen Mary* began in 1959 and a modernised version of 75,000 tons was first envisaged—a liner akin to *France* [148] but berthing three passenger Classes. The British Government promised generous financial aid and tenders were invited four years later. By then, however, the impossibility of such a ship competing profitably with air-travel in winter had become all too obvious and the projected new '*Queen*' was dropped in favour of an entirely different vessel. The Cunard fell back on the example which the Canadian Pacific had set with the *Empress of Britain* of 1931—an outstanding dual-purpose ship, equal to the finest of the regular transatlantic liners and yet specifically designed for long-distance winter cruising. The cruising factor limited size, but also allowed some reduction in power since no reserve was needed to meet winter North Atlantic weather conditions. So different was the liner ordered from the one originally contemplated that the company were at pains to stress that she would not be a '*Queen*' as then understood. Government assistance was again obtained and the unnamed vessel, later to be called *Queen Elizabeth 2*, laid down 5 July 1965. *Queen Elizabeth*, a better appointed ship than *Queen Mary*, was refitted to give her another 10 years' life so that she could run in concert with the dual-purpose liner. Southampton–New York sailings had already been cut to fortnightly for four months a year, but the volume of seaborne transatlantic passenger traffic continued to decline and monetary losses to mount. So the decision was reached in 1967 to employ only one ship even in summer. *Queen Mary* was retired that year and *Queen Elizabeth* at close of the 1968 season. Plans for their successor underwent some modification and the Cunard Company adopted the idea that, when employed on the North Atlantic, she should provide a holiday-with-transport instead of an alternative to air-transport. *Queen Elizabeth 2* was therefore fitted out with amenities on a scale previously unknown in any transatlantic or even cruising liner.

The new ship took her maiden sailing from Southampton for New York, 2 May 1969. She calls at Havre in place of Cherbourg and occasionally puts into Cobh. Arrangements have been made with the Cie. Gle. Transatlantique for *Queen Elizabeth 2* and *France* to sail for New York alternate weeks.

The Cunard is head of a shipping group based on Liverpool, although headquarters of the Cunard Line itself were transferred to

Southampton in July 1966. The passenger fleet has dwindled to three units of which *Carmania* and *Franconia* have become regular cruising liners, but their programmes entail stray Atlantic passages. This decline has been offset by increased attention to cargo and the original cargo fleet entirely replaced. The company has also combined with the Cie. Gle. Transatlantique, the Holland–America Line, the Swedish American and two smaller concerns to form the Atlantic Container Lines consortium which has a fleet of ten ships built or building. The Cunard's passenger and cargo interests have been separated by transferring the three passenger liners to a subsidiary company called Cunard Line, Ltd.

The former White Star ships *Adriatic*, *Albertic* and *Calgaric*, were taken over by the Cunard and not broken up until 1934–35 although never used. They have therefore been omitted from the fleet-list.

[1] *MAURETANIA* 1907–35 Swan Hunter
30,700t. 762 × 88 4–2 T–4 25½k.

The classic *Mauretania* made her fastest crossing after conversion from coal to oil-firing—5d. 1h. 49m. (26·25 knots) from the Ambrose to Cherbourg in 1924. Five years afterwards she lost the Atlantic 'Blue Riband'. By 1933 *Mauretania* had been painted white and her only transatlantic passages were then in connection with pleasure-cruising from New York. The last of these commenced on 26 Sept. 1934 and occupied 5d. 0h. 20m. to Plymouth (24·4 knots). She left Southampton for Rosyth shipbreakers, July 1935.

[2] *AQUITANIA* 1914–49 Brown
45,650t. 868 × 97 4–2 T–4 23½k.

The most handsome of the coal-burning 'giants', *Aquitania* (597 First, 614 Second, 2052 Third) was ordered to maintain a three-ship weekly service in conjunction with *Lusitania* and *Mauretania*. She had completed only three New York voyages from the Mersey when requisitioned. Conversion to an armed merchant cruiser was abandoned, but she served as troopship, hospital ship and again troopship in turn. Reconditioning in 1920 was accompanied by alteration of furnaces from coal-firing to oil. Best crossing of the decade was at 23·62 knots from the Ambrose to Cherbourg. From 1936 it became necessary to make *Aquitania* as adequate a running-mate as possible for *Queen Mary* and squeeze the maximum speed out of her. Finest performances between Cherbourg and the Ambrose were made that year—5d. 10h. 6m. (24·82 knots) outward and 5d. 8h. 17m. (24·87) eastward—and 24-knot passages became regular.

Aquitania commenced World War II trooping in 1939 and helped bring the first Canadian contingent to Great Britain. Later she carried Australians to Egypt and finally Americans to Europe. On completion of trooping the Ministry of Transport retained *Aquitania* to take emigrants to Halifax. The

Cunard recovered possession of their veteran in March 1948, but found her not worth reconditioning. So she resumed the Southampton-Halifax sailings with 'austerity' accommodation after the minimum overhaul. This second series was subsidised by the Canadian Government and ended at Southampton, 1 Dec. 1949.

[3]	*BERENGARIA* ('13)	1921–38	Hamburg (Vulkan)

52,000t. 883 × 98 3–2* T–4 23k.

Berengaria started as *Imperator*, the first of three giant liners ordered by the Hamburg–American company (*see Leviathan* [83]). She was surrendered to the victorious Allies after World War I and operated under charter by the Cunard in 1920. The following year the Cunard and the White Star combined to buy *Imperator* and *Bismarck* (*see Majestic* [18]) from the British Government to avoid bidding against each other. Each took one vessel and joint-ownership continued for 10 years.

The Cunard Line re-registered *Imperator* as *Berengaria*. Reconditioning included conversion to an oil-burner and raised speed from 22½ knots to 23. The ex-German ship joined *Mauretania* and *Aquitania* in the Southampton–New York service, April 1922, and made her fastest passages the same year—23¼ knots westbound and 23¾ home. Alteration of accommodation to 970 First, 630 Second, 515 Tourist and 606 Third was typical of the changes made in most North Atlantic liners during the later 1920's. Merging of the Cunard and White Star lines brought *Berengaria* and *Majestic* under the same house-flag, but *Berengaria* was considered the better ship and *Majestic* sold out of the fleet. The ex-*Imperator* completed her final voyage in March 1938, was partly dismantled at Jarrow and the hull towed to the Forth in 1946 for final scrapping.

[4]	*SCYTHIA*	1921–57	Barrow
[5]	*SAMARIA*	1922–55	Birkenhead
[6]	*LACONIA*	1922–42	Swan Hunter

19,700t. 607 × 73 1–2 GT–2 16k.

347 First, 350 Second, 1500 Third. Five sisterships were simultaneously contracted for, but work on two suspended and eventually finished to a slightly modified design. The fourth unit, *Franconia* [11], always sailed in partnership with the earlier vessels and her career is best described under the same heading. The *Scythia*s and *Franconia* maintained the Cunard's Liverpool–Cobh–New York sailings until beginning of World War II.

Samaria and *Franconia* were requisitioned as troop-transports in 1939; *Scythia* later. *Laconia* began hostilities as an armed merchant cruiser, but subsequently joined the others trooping. In December 1939 the westbound *Samaria* was routed too close to the track of the first eastbound Canadian troop convoy and collided with H.M.S. *Furious* and *Aquitania* in turn. *Scythia* remained afloat after being torpedoed from the air off Algiers, 23 Nov. 1942. *Laconia* met her end by torpedo from '*U.156*' 260 miles north-east of Ascension on 12 Sept. 1942. She was carrying 2732 persons, including 1500 Italian prisoners and some women passengers. The survivors numbered 1111 and would have been far fewer but for events which were only fully explained years afterwards. '*U.156*' identified Italians in the lifeboats and asked German Submarine Headquarters in Paris for instructions. She was told to make every effort to save life, and '*U.506*' and '*U.507*' left their patrols to assist. The three submarines collected the lifeboats together, took casualties on board, etc. The French despatched the cruiser *Gloire* from Dakar. She reached the scene five nights after the sinking, embarked survivors and landed them at Dakar. Unfortunately an American aircraft from Ascension had bombed the submarines while rescue work was in progress and German submarine commanders inevitably received instructions not to attempt to save life in future.

Franconia was released in 1949; *Scythia* and *Samaria* next year. They were re-conditioned to carry 250 First and 600–640 Tourist Class passengers and used for Canadian sailings in conjunction with *Ascania* [14]. Draught prevented proceeding beyond Quebec and, as it was, *Franconia* grounded in the St. Lawrence on 12 July 1950. Tugs refloated her four days later, but a large hole necessitated repair before return home. *Scythia* and *Samaria* usually worked from Southampton and *Franconia* from Liverpool, although the latter made nine voyages from Greenock in 1954. *Scythia* sheered the stern off the Canadian collier *Wabana* in fog below Quebec, 5 June 1952.

Samaria remained in the Southampton–Canada trade to the last. *Franconia* was moved to Southampton in June 1955. The following April an engine defect forced her to return to the Hampshire port when two days out and abandonment of the voyage. After repair she went back to her pre-war Liverpool–Cobh–New York route and *Scythia*'s last year was also spent in this service.

[7]	*ANDANIA*	1922–40	Hawthorn Leslie
[8]	*ANTONIA*	1922–40	Barrow
[9]	*AUSCONIA*	1922–39	Tyne (Vickers)

13,900t. 520 × 65 1–2 GT–2 15k.

These three Cabin Class liners belonged to a group of six ordered simultaneously for the St. Lawrence trade. *See Aurania* [13].

[10]	*LANCASTRIA* ('22)	1924–40	Beardmore

16,250t. 552 × 70 1–2 GT–2 16k.

An odd unit in the Cunard fleet (*see* Anchor *Cameronia* [61]). *Lancastria* began at *Tyrrhenia*, a 3-Class liner which was converted to Cabin after two years and renamed. Her only commercial employment from 1932 onwards was pleasure-cruising.

Requisitioning, September 1939, was for trooping. Loss of *Lancastria* at anchor off St. Nazaire on 17 June 1940 ranks as the worst British troopship disaster. She was about to leave when attacked by dive-bombers. Three bombs burst inside the ship, wreaking frightful havoc among the 6000 men crammed on board. Exits were blocked and *Lancastria* foundered 20 minutes after the onslaught. Some 3000 troops perished but the exact number could never be established.

[11]	*FRANCONIA*	1923–56	Brown
[12]	*CARINTHIA*	1925–40	Barrow

20,200t. 601 × 73 1–2 GT–2 16k.

Delayed units of the *Scythia* class with accommodation for 240 First, 460 Second and 950 Third, and the bridge joined to the main superstructure instead of being isolated. *Franconia* often cruised during the winter, but her career is recorded under *Scythia* [4]. *Carinthia* was laid down as *Servia* and renamed on resumption of work after lengthy suspension. She was fitted out as a long-distance cruising-liner, though she made regular summer voyages to New York during her earlier years. *Carinthia* was among the first liners taken for conversion to armed merchant cruisers in 1939 and had a serious collision with *Circassia*, another liner-cruiser. She struck *Circassia* forward of the bridge and penetrated almost to the centre-line. *Carinthia* fell victim to '*U.46*' off Northern Ireland, 6 June 1940.

[13]	*AURANIA*	1924–39	Swan Hunter
[14]	*ASCANIA*	1925–56	Tyne (Vickers)
[15]	*ALAUNIA*	1925–39	Brown

14,000t. 520 × 65 1–2 GT–2 15k.

Second batch of the *Andania* sextette. Work on these steamers was suspended and recommenced after an interval as in the case of *Franconia* and *Carinthia*. Differences between the *Andania*s and the *Aurania*s were confined to the superstructure which in the *Andania*s was of the island-type. Each ship berthed 500 Cabin and 1200 Third. Employment was entirely in the Canadian services. Two (usually *Andania* and *Antonia*) maintained fortnightly sailings from Liverpool and the others weekly from London. Primary concern of the *Andania*s and *Aurania*s was freight and their length the maximum the Surrey Commercial Docks allowed. They proved popular with shippers of cargo paying the highest rates, but from a passenger standpoint compared poorly with rival Canadian Pacific liners. The only one to attract public attention was *Ascania* which on 14 Dec. 1934 rescued the crew of the sinking tramp steamer *Usworth* in a mid-Atlantic gale. *Ascania* was refloated without difficulty after grounding 150 miles below Quebec, 2 July 1938.

Five of the six commissioned as liner-cruisers in September 1939, but *Antonia* was not requisitioned until needed for trooping, October 1940. The ex-Turkish submarine '*UA*' torpedoed *Andania*, 15 June 1940, 70 miles south of Reykjavik and the British vessel sank the following morning. *Aurania* collided with an iceberg, July 1941, while escorting a Halifax convoy. The Admiralty bought four of the class for conversion to naval repair ships—*Antonia* and *Aurania* in March 1942; *Ausonia*, July 1942; *Alaunia*, December 1944. The first pair were renamed *Wayland* and *Artifex* respectively, and lasted until 1948 and 1960. *Ausonia* went to breakers in 1965 and *Alaunia* in 1957.

Ascania carried troops from 1943 onwards. She received the briefest of overhauls after release and cleared Liverpool for Halifax on 20 Dec. 1947. Full reconditioning with 198 First Class berths and 498 Tourist was deferred until the 1949–50 winter. Until *Saxonia* [30] joined the fleet *Ascania* was the only Cunard passenger liner proceeding upstream from Quebec to Montreal. From September 1955 she was based on Southampton instead of Liverpool.

[16] *OLYMPIC* ('11) 1934–35 Belfast
46,450t. 852 × 92 4–2* 3ET–3 21½k.

Olympic and the six ships which follow were former White Star liners.

The White Star ordered three sisters of abnormal size with just enough speed to provide a weekly service between them, but only *Olympic* ever reached New York. *Titanic* foundered on her maiden passage and *Britannic* was sunk by mine in the Aegean without taking a commercial sailing. *Olympic*, earliest of the group, had her watertight subdivision improved after the *Titanic* disaster and was converted to oil-burning in 1920. She rammed and sank two ships during her career, one seeking to destroy her and the second to aid. On 12 May 1918 *Olympic* sank the German submarine '*U.103*' and on 16 May 1934 the Nantucket Lightship in thick fog. The Cunard withdrew *Olympic* from service the following March.

[17] *HOMERIC* ('22) 1934–36 Danzig
34,350t. 751 × 83 2–2 3E–2 19½k.

The first of two German vessels which the White Star bought to partner *Olympic*. *Homeric* was a virtual sister of *Columbus* [182]. Changing her from a coal-burner to oil in 1923–24 improved original speed of 18½ although this still remained inadequate. *Homeric*'s last New York voyage was in January 1932 and subsequent employment cruising to the Mediterranean and West Indies for the White Star and Cunard.

[18] *MAJESTIC* ('22) 1934–36 Hamburg (Blohm & Voss)
56,600t. 915 × 100 3–2* T–4 23½k.

The White Star *Majestic* was the largest ship afloat until the French *Normandie* of 1935 and the last of three big liners ordered by the Hamburg-American Line (*see Leviathan* [83]). Her German name was *Bismarck* and she was finished as an oil-fired ship. Best authenticated passage-time was 5d. 5h. 21m. (24·76 knots) from the Ambrose to Cherbourg in 1923. Unfortunately *Majestic* showed structural weakness the year following. Passenger complement on transfer to the Cunard was 860 First, 705 Tourist Class and 626 Third.

Majestic's last Atlantic voyage ended in February 1936. Shipbreakers bought the former White Star liner and resold her almost immediately to the Admiralty. Masts and funnels were cut down and *Majestic* became the boys' training-ship *Caledonia*, stationed at Rosyth. Machinery and boilers were left intact. Her boys were transferred elsewhere when war started and extensive alterations planned. These can only have meant restoration to seagoing condition for trooping, although this was never promulgated and the ship destroyed before work had started. On 29 Sept. 1939 fire broke out on board and the ex-*Majestic* sank under the weight of the water pumped into her. She settled on the bottom in an upright position, was held a total loss and dismantled as far as possible where she lay. What remained of the hull was refloated in 1943 and broken up locally.

[19] *DORIC* ('23) 1934–35 Belfast
16,500t. 575 × 68 2–2* GT–2 15½k.

An excellent little Cabin Class liner built for the White Star's Canadian service and virtually a turbine-driven version of *Pennland* [207]. From 1933 *Doric* was used exclusively for cruising. On 5 Sept. 1935 she collided with the French *Formigny* off Vigo and was so badly damaged that she went to scrappers on arrival home.

[20] *LAURENTIC* ('27) 1934–40 Belfast
18,700t. 578 × 75 2–2 3ET–2 16k.

Laurentic (594 Cabin, 318 Tourist Class, 303 Third) represented a retrogressive step on *Doric* as regards firing and main machinery. She was the last North Atlantic passenger liner of any company to be either a coal-burner or propelled by reciprocating engines. *Laurentic* ran steadily to Canada to the end of the White Star regime and also made a few Canadian voyages for the Cunard. Later employment was restricted to cruising and she was so employed when struck by *Napier Star* off the Skerries on 18 August 1935. A hole was torn in her side and she lost six of her crew. *Laurentic* made a trooping trip to Palestine towards the end of 1936 and the Cunard laid the ship up on her return home. The only reason for retaining the former White Star liner was having a coal-fired ship in reserve as an insurance against a possible oil-fuel shortage. At outbreak of World War II *Laurentic* was fitted out for service as an armed merchant cruiser. She was torpedoed and sunk by '*U.99*' near Bloody Foreland on 4 Nov. 1940.

[21] *BRITANNIC* ('30) 1934–60
[22] *GEORGIC* ('32) 1934–40 } Belfast
GEORGIC (0) 1950–54
26,950t./27,750t. 680 × 82 2-2* M–2 18k.

479 Cabin Class, 557 Tourist and 506 Third in excellent quarters. *Britannic* and *Georgic* were the only British passenger motorships ever built for the North Atlantic and differed slightly in external appearance. The White Star Line used them on the Liverpool–Cobh–New York route, but the Cunard moved the pair to the London–Havre–Southampton–New York in April 1935.

Requisitioning of *Britannic* in September 1939 was for trooping and her sister taken for the same purpose the following March. *Georgic* was burned out at Port Tewfik (Suez Canal) as a result of air attack, but subsequently salved from a half-submerged position and brought back to Belfast. The Ministry of Transport bought the wreck in March 1943 and rebuilt *Georgic* as a regular troop transport. Reconstruction included removal of the mainmast and replacing the two funnels with a single one. The Ministry placed her under Cunard management and White Star colours.

Britannic was reconditioned to carry 429 First Class and 564 Tourist travellers and restored to the Liverpool–Cobh–New York trade in Mav 1948. She sailed without a partner and cruised from New York each winter. *Georgic*, which had been adapted for taking government-sponsored emigrants to Australia in the late 1940's was chartered by the Cunard for six or seven New York voyages every summer from 1950 till 1954, charging Tourist Class fares. The first year she sailed from Liverpool; the remainder, from Southampton. She was sold to shipbreakers in 1955. *Britannic* finished her last voyage on 2 Dec. 1960.

[23] *QUEEN MARY* 1936–67 Brown
80,750t. 965 × 119 3–2 GT–4 29½k.

Queen Mary was the last Western Ocean record-breaker built entirely at owners' expense and operated without a subsidy. Government loans were made to facilitate her construction but all repaid on time. Length between perpendiculars by the pre-1955 rules was 975 feet and she measured 1020 overall. Gross tonnage underwent minor increases as more space was enclosed and *Queen Mary*'s final figure was 81,250.

In 1929 the Norddeutscher Lloyd *Bremen* completely out-stripped the 22-year-old *Mauretania* and the Cunard Steam-Ship Company lost the speed-supremacy it had held so long. *Mauretania* was approaching the end of her days and the time had arrived to plan a replacement. If regular 4½-day crossings were made the target, her successor and a similar vessel would be capable of the same number of sailings as the existing three (*Mauretania*, *Aquitania* and *Berengaria*). The required increase in speed would mean two liners over half as big again as the German record-breaker and their cost be enormous, but the resulting two-ship weekly service judged financially sound. The Cunard directors therefore decided to build one 4½-day ship to relieve *Mauretania*, follow her up with a second and then retire *Berengaria* and *Aquitania*. Keel of the first was laid on 27 Dec. 1930, but no name allocated and she was referred to by her works number, '534'.

Construction of '534' began at an unfortunate moment, for the early 1930's brought one of the worst depressions shipping has ever known. The Cunard Company was compelled to conserve its financial resources and suspended construction on 10 Dec. 1931. After an interval the British Government offered to lend £3 million on very favourable terms to complete '534' and £5 million to provide a consort, on condition that the Cunard Line amalgamated with the White Star. There was no practical alternative to acceptance. Work recommenced in April 1934 and the ship was launched on 26 Sept. of that year. The name contemplated is believed to have been *Queen Victoria*, a new style and yet incorporating the Cunard suffix '–IA', but the hull slid into the Clyde as *Queen Mary*.

Mean speed on trials worked out at 32·84 knots and *Queen Mary* cleared Southampton for New York, 27 May 1936. Her rival, *Normandie*, had been built with government assistance from the start and construction proceeded without a break. Consequently the French liner had 12 months' running before the Cunarder's maiden voyage. Differences between the two ships in size and speed were very small, but the British was propelled by single-reduction geared turbines and *Normandie* by turbo-electric machinery. *Queen Mary* gave greater attention to passengers at the less-expensive fares than the French vessel and carried 776 Cabin Class, 784 Tourist and 579 Third. Rating *Queen Mary*'s best accommodation Cabin threatened to disrupt the North Atlantic Passenger Conference. Despite a vast improvement in the Cabin Class standard this category had never before been associated with a vessel of outstanding speed. Upshot of the Cunard action was abolition of the terms 'First' and 'Second', and general substitution of 'Cabin Class' to cover both.

Use of steam at much higher pressure than *Berengaria* caused *Queen Mary's* daily oil consumption to amount to little more than the older ship's. The new Cunarder made no attempt to beat *Normandie's* records until her sixth voyage and then succeeded in both directions. The French liner improved on the British times the following year and *Queen Mary* claimed still better in 1938. The shortest passages between Bishop Rock and the Ambrose Lightship and the speeds claimed are set out below—

BISHOP ROCK—AMBROSE

		d.	h.	m.	k.
1935	*Normandie*	4	3	14	(29·94)
1936	*Queen Mary*	4	0	27	(30·14)
1937	*Normandie*	3	23	2	(30·58)
1938	*Queen Mary*	3	21	48	(30·99)

AMBROSE—BISHOP ROCK

		d.	h.	m.	k.
1935	*Normandie*	4	3	28	(30·31)
1936	*Queen Mary*	3	23	57	(30·63)
1937	*Normandie*	4	0	6	(30·99)
1937	,,	3	22	7	(31·20)
1938	*Queen Mary*	3	20	42	(31·69)

Various factors such as the vagaries of weather and the track-mileages claimed allow no more than a broad interpretation of these figures, but such advantage as one rival may have possessed over the other, lay with *Queen Mary*.

Declaration of war on Germany found Britain's largest liner approaching New York, where she was laid up on arrival. Shortage of tonnage soon necessitated sending *Queen Mary* to Sydney for conversion to a troopship. She left the Hudson on 21 March 1940 and proceeded round the Cape. Her War career included extensive employment carrying Australian and New Zealand troops to Egypt and other theatres. After the United States' entry into the war *Queen Mary* reverted to the North Atlantic for moving American troops to Europe. She and *Queen Elizabeth* between them accounted for 320,500 of the 865,000 members of the American armed forces landed in Britain up to the German surrender. Both were based on the Clyde port of Gourock. Each carried as many as 15,000 men across the Atlantic at a time except during the winter months when the number was reduced to 10,500 to improve stability. Bunks had to be shared, some troops sleeping while others moved about the ship. *Queen Mary* was never attacked by either submarine or aircraft, but a major tragedy marred her transport work. She was off Bloody Foreland on the morning of 2 Oct. 1942 when the anti-aircraft cruiser *Curacoa* joined her escort. *Queen Mary* was the faster of the two and difficulties arose from the desirability of the escorting cruiser stationing herself ahead. As the troopship came out of a zigzag *Curacoa* tried to dart across her bow but failed. Some 100 feet were clipped clean off aft and sank immediately; the rest of the warship stayed afloat about 20 minutes. 338 lives were lost in the disaster. *Queen Mary* escaped with nothing worse than a badly twisted stem, but had to reduce speed to 13 knots for the rest of her passage to the Clyde. Lengthy and unsatisfactory litigation which followed ended with the troopship being held one-third to blame.

After victory had been won in Europe *Queen Mary* ferried troops back to New York and finally the wives and families of Canadian soldiers to Halifax. Voyages under requisition ended at Southampton on 27 Sept. 1946 with a 3d. 15h. 48m. passage from Halifax (29 knots). The merging of First and Second Classes did not survive the 1939–45 War and *Queen Mary* was reconditioned to take 711 First, 707 Second and 577 Tourist. She resumed commercial employment on her old run, 31 July 1947. The fitting of stabilizing fins was delayed until the 1957–58 winter because of technical difficulties arising from her large boiler rooms. *Queen Mary* kept the Atlantic speed-record until eclipsed by *United States* in 1952, but attempts at outstandingly swift crossings were pointless in the post-war period and her best passages attributable to need to recover time because of delays in port. The press credited *Queen Mary* with averaging 30 knots on an April 1962 4d. 9h. 51m. passage from the Ambrose to Cherbourg, but a mean speed of 29·46 on a 4d. 10h. 6m. passage between the same points (4d. 3h. 0m. from Ambrose to the Bishop) in August 1966 which was also acclaimed her post-war best is more acceptable.

Some small reduction in the number of berths took place in *Queen Mary*'s closing years. From 1963–64 she spent part of each winter short-distance pleasure-cruising, usually from Southampton. On 9 Dec. 1965 *Queen Mary* stood by the distressed Greek *Konstantis* in a gale 300 miles south-west of Ireland, but the freighter managed to reach port. Stabilizing fins had been fitted in 1958 (three years after *Queen Elizabeth* because of the larger boiler-rooms creating technical difficulties) and the Cunard had planned to keep *Queen Mary* running until *Queen Elizabeth 2*'s completion, but she was offered for sale after the 1967 decision to curtail New York sailings to fortnightly.

Thousands of Americans had known this famous liner during her trooping years and this brought offers to buy from many communities who wished to preserve her. Success went to the City of Long Beach who paid a little under £1¼ million and took delivery on 21 Oct. 1967. Final departure from New York had been on 22 Sept. and the Hudson River is unlikely ever again to see so stately a ship. *Queen Mary* made two cruises to the Canaries after return to Southampton and then proceeded to California round Cape Horn under Cunard management, carrying passengers and putting into intermediate ports. Her active career finished just before noon, 9 Dec. 1967, when she berthed alongside at Long Beach. That morning she had been escorted up harbour by an armada consisting of 10 Navy minesweepers, 96 Coast Guard vessels, 6 tugs, 2 fireboats and an estimated 5000 private small craft. Overhead flew more than 100 aeroplanes and a blimp airship. No welcome could have been more stupendous and it marked the end of an era. *Queen Mary* has been converted to a maritime museum with one engine-room kept in approximately original condition and enough boiler-power retained to turn one propeller. The first and third funnels have been removed.

[24] *MAURETANIA* 1939–65 Birkenhead

35,750t. 733 × 89 2–2 GT–2 23k.

An excellent liner which had the misfortune to be completely overshadowed by the two '*Queens*'. She and her famous namesake were the only fast Cunarders ever ordered away from the Clyde. *Mauretania* was ordered to augment the London–New York sailings of the two *Britannics* and cruise from New York over the winter months. Speed was relatively high so that she could relieve a '*Queen*' in an emergency although this contingency never arose. The contract was placed after *Queen Elizabeth* and work proceeded so fast that the ship was completed in two years. *Mauretania*'s maiden passage began at Liverpool, 17 June 1939. She returned to London and made two New York voyages from there. The fourth homeward crossing brought her back to the Mersey. *Mauretania* waited several weeks at Liverpool and then sailed for New York where she was laid up until March 1940.

Mauretania was requisitioned and routed through the Panama Canal to Sydney for fitting out as a troopship. Until April 1943 she was variously employed moving troops between Australia, India, Egypt, North Africa and Britain. During the next two years *Mauretania* carried Americans and Canadians to Europe, but after Germany's surrender was generally used between Liverpool and Indian Ocean ports, although in 1945 she circled the globe via Panama and Capetown (28,650 miles) in 81½ days.

Reconditioning at Birkenhead occupied seven months and this ship cleared Liverpool for New York on 26 April 1947 with 475 First, 390 Second and 304 Tourist Class berths. Southampton became her British terminal with her third post-war sailing. *Mauretania* operated a New York service of her own via Havre and Cobh for seven–eight months a year and cruised during the winter. Best crossings were 5d. 12h. 30m. (24·33 knots) from Ambrose to Liverpool and 5d. 1h. 56m. (23·85) from Cobh to Ambrose in 1947 and 1948 respectively. She was a popular ship, attracting travellers who would otherwise have booked in the '*Queens*' and the effect of this became serious as passenger traffic declined. So she was scheduled for ten New York–Cannes–Genoa–Naples voyages to follow her 1962–63 winter cruising programme. The experiment was not a success and the last two voyages were cancelled. Winter cruising for 1963–64 was from Southampton and *Mauretania* was then restored to her old Southampton–New York route. In 1965 she was used only for cruising although this included two Southampton–New York passages. *Mauretania* left Southampton on the second of these, 4 Aug., cruised in the Eastern Mediterranean and went to shipbreakers immediately after her return home. Sale for scrapping was premature, but profitable employment lacking.

[25] *QUEEN ELIZABETH* ('40) 1946–68 Brown

83,650t. 965 × 118 2–2 GT–4 29½k.

Consort for *Queen Mary* and the largest passenger liner ever built. Machinery and power were similar, but improvements in boiler design permitted the number of boilers to be reduced from 24 to 12, thereby saving space and abolishing one funnel. Hull changes were small. A more pronounced rake on the stem increased length overall to 1031 feet and between perpendiculars under the old rules to 987. The well forward was omitted and a third anchor added. Alterations in internal layout were considerable. *Queen Elizabeth* was laid down 4 Dec. 1936 and launched 27 Sept. 1938. Her maiden voyage was announced as commencing on 24 April 1940, but outbreak of war rendered completion to the original plans pointless and the desirability of moving the unfinished ship beyond reach of enemy bombers obvious. *Queen Elizabeth* therefore slipped secretly down the Clyde as soon as she could be made ready for sea and arrived at New York, 7 March 1940 after a 24½-knot crossing.

Queen Elizabeth stayed alongside at New York until 12 Nov. 1940 when despatched to Singapore. There she was fitted for trooping before joining *Queen Mary*, *Aquitania* and others in carrying men between Australia, New Zealand, Malaya, India and Africa. The Indian Ocean was then relatively safe for such valuable ships, but after Japanese entry into the war they were shifted to the Atlantic for ferrying United States troops to the Clyde. *See Queen Mary*. On a westward crossing with women and children evacuated to North America *Queen Elizabeth* was attacked by '*U.704*' 200 miles from Ireland. Four torpedoes were fired and missed.

De-requisitioning came in March 1946 and the builders at once took the ship in hand, equipping her as a luxury liner for 823 First Class, 662 Second and 798 Tourist passengers. Most of the work was done at Southampton, but some on the Clyde. Fitting *Queen Elizabeth* out as a 3-Class ship from the start and the extra space gave her superior accommodation to *Queen Mary*. Tourist Class quarters and the crew's living spaces were markedly better. On 25 Oct. 1946 she left Southampton on her first commercial voyage to New York. If she had been given the same chance to show her paces as *Queen Mary*, the newer ship would probably have shown herself equally speedy, but by 1946 her machinery had already seen five years' use. Oil consumption was higher. *Queen Elizabeth*'s best performance came in 1954—Ambrose to Bishop Rock in 4d. 5h. 3m. (29·77 knots).

Queen Elizabeth was fitted with stabilizing fins during her 1954–55 refit and needed a double-set because of her length. On 29 July 1959 she inflicted serious damage on the freighter *American Hunter* in collision in the Ambrose Channel but escaped lightly herself. A very extensive refit in 1965–66 gave her another 10 years of active life with berths for 704 First, 664 Second and 627 Tourist passengers. Object of the refit had been to enable *Queen Elizabeth* to run in tandem with *Queen Mary*'s replacement well into the 1970's, but she was offered for sale in 1968 during which year she made her Southampton–New York voyages without a companion.

As in the case of *Queen Mary* there were many offers to buy *Queen Elizabeth* for preservation in some form or other. She was in very much better condition than her former consort. A Philadelphia syndicate undertook to pay nearly £3¼ million and berth her in the Delaware as a convention and hotel ship, but the transaction fell through.

Queen Elizabeth was eventually sold in July, 1969, to a U.S. firm called The Queen, Ltd., who plan to transform the ship into an array of shops, theatres and restaurants together with hotel and convention facilities which will make it one of the outstanding resort and convention centres in the United States. The ship will be anchored at Fort Lauderdale/Hollywood area of Florida.

[26]	*MEDIA*	1947–61	Brown
[27]	*PARTHIA*	1948–61	Belfast

13,350t. 601 × 70 1–1 GT–2 17½k.

Earliest post-war passenger liners built for any North Atlantic company, *Media* and *Parthia* carried one Class of passenger in spacious quarters and were a new style of ship for the Cunard. Fare for the 250 First Class passengers stood closer to Second in the *Queens* than the First in *Saxonia* [29]. A single mast stepped far forward gave them an unusual profile. The two ships sailed directly between the Mersey and New York, and made a few homeward passages at 18 knots. They were poor seaboats and fitted with stabilizing fins after a year or two, being the first Atlantic liners so equipped.

Media and her sister were sold to other operators at the end of 1961. The Cogedar Line of Genoa bought *Media* for their Australian emigrant service and renamed her *Flavia.* At the end of 1968 she was chartered to operate between Miami and Nassau. The P. & O. Group feared that *Parthia* might go to a competitor and therefore bought the ship although they had no real use for her. She is now the Eastern & Australian Company's *Aramac* after three years with the New Zealand Shipping Company as *Remuera.*

[28]	*CARONIA*	1949–68	Brown

34,200t. 666 × 91 1–1 GT–2 22k.

Primarily a long-distance cruising-liner, although intended to partner *Mauretania* for a few New York voyages at the height of the season. *Caronia* and *Mauretania* were of much the same size, but their proportions could hardly have been more different and *Caronia* was one of the 'stumpiest' liners ever built. Purpose of the reduced length was to facilitate entry into difficult harbours. The cruising factor led to omission of Tourist Class accommodation. *Caronia* berthed 580 First and 350 Second, and the two Classes were combined on cruises. The Cunard Company emphasised this ship's special character by painting the hull green instead of black.

Cruises were always from New York and *Caronia* cleared Southampton 4 Jan. 1949 to commence her career as a dollar-earner. She made three or four transatlantic voyages each summer in her first years, but later crossings became incidental to cruising schedules. The one notable episode in her career was at Yokohama on 14 April 1958. The tugs helping her out of harbour suddenly ceased their efforts and *Caronia* crashed into the mole, tearing a six-foot gash in her bow in the process. *Caronia* proved a highly successful investment, but bookings fell away as she aged and competition in the long-distance cruising fleld intensified. An extensive 1965–66 refit failed to restore the ship to favour and she was taken out of service in November 1967. A projected purchase for use as a floating hotel at Dubrovnik fell through, but in May the Universal Line of Panama bought her. *Caronia* has been re-registered as *Columbia* and the new owners plan to give her a big refit as a prelude to further cruising.

[29] *STRATHEDEN* ('38) (0) 1950 23,700t. 640 × 82 1–2 GT–2 20k.

A P. & O. liner chartered for four summer Southampton–Havre–New York voyages.

[30]	*SAXONIA*	1954	Brown
	CARMANIA	1963–	
[31]	*IVERNIA*	1955	
	FRANCONIA	1963–	

21,650t. 570 × 80 1–1 GT–2 20k.

Built as sisters of *Carinthia* and *Sylvania* (below) for the Montreal service and their early history appears under these ships.

General decline in the Canadian passenger trade caused *Saxonia* and *Ivernia* to be temporarily withdrawn at the end of 1962 for reconstruction by the builders as dual-purpose liners. The after-holds were eliminated, extra public rooms fitted and cabins remodelled to accommodate 118 travellers in the First Class and 736 in the Tourist. Tonnage rose to 22,600 gross, hulls were painted the cruising colour of *Caronia* and the ships renamed. *Carmania* was finished in April 1963 and *Ivernia* two months later. The pair returned to the Southampton–Montreal service, but winter employment became cruising from American ports. Nearly half their Canadian voyages began at Rotterdam with a Southampton call.

At the beginning of 1967 *Franconia* sailed from England to inaugurate a regular New York–Bermuda service and *Sylvania* [33] partnered *Carmania* in the Rotterdam/Southampton Canadian trade that summer. At the end of the season the Cunard Steam-Ship Company abandoned the Canadian passenger business and *Carmania* has since been used entirely for pleasure-cruises from European or American ports. Her December 1968 cruise from Port Everglades was cancelled because of a dispute with the American authorities about compliance with new fire-safety regulations. On 11 Jan. 1969 she grounded off Watling Island and was refloated by tugs six days later. *Carmania* dry-docked at Newport News and was unable to resume her cruising until 8 Feb.

[32]	*CARINTHIA*	1956–67	Brown
[33]	*SYLVANIA*	1957–68	

21,950t. 570 × 80 1–1 GT–2 20k.

Despite some differences in internal arrangements *Saxonia, Ivernia, Carinthia* and *Sylvania* were sisterships and formed the largest block of passenger liners ordered by a North Atlantic company for many years. They were the first Canadian passenger vessels built since *Empress of Britain* of 1931 and as good as any Canadian Pacific tonnage. The initial contract was for two ships and *Carinthia* ordered a year later. Subsequent addition of *Sylvania*, allowing four sailings every three weeks, came as rather a surprise. Draught gave these liners the access to Montreal which had been denied the *Scythia*s. Passenger complements of the first pair were 110 First and 820 Tourist, and the second carried 150 and 715. Many cabins were interchangeable.

Each ship began by working from the Mersey. *Carinthia* relieved *Ivernia* in June 1956 and *Sylvania* displaced *Saxonia* 12 months afterwards. The older pair then settled down on the Southampton route which gave the Cunard a Canadian sailing from Liverpool one week, from Southampton the next and from both ports every third week. Some of *Saxonia*'s and *Ivernia*'s winter voyages started at London and skipped Southampton, but otherwise this arrangement lasted until the end of 1960. *Sylvania* then took the place of *Britannic* in the Liverpool–Cobh–New York trade and called at Halifax during the winter. Later history of *Saxonia* and *Ivernia* appears under their separate heading.

Carinthia worked steadily between Liverpool and Canada except for occasional Southampton winter sailings after conversion of the *Saxonia* couple to dual-purpose liners, and two or three short winter cruises in later years. She finished with two, Southampton–Montreal voyages and was offered for sale, December 1967. *Sylvania*'s 1964–65 New York voyages included some Boston calls. Her departure from the Mersey on 24 Nov. 1966 ended the Liverpool–New York passenger sailings which the Cunard had commenced in 1848. *Sylvania* ran between Southampton and Montreal the next season in partnership with *Carmania* (ex-*Saxonia*) and on 15 July grounded below Quebec. She was westbound and refloated undamaged after four days. Final Atlantic crossing was ex-Montreal on 28 Oct. 1967. Some short cruises from British ports followed, although *Sylvania* and *Carinthia* were offered for sale simultaneously. The Sitmar Line bought both ships at the beginning of 1968, but delivery of *Sylvania* was deferred to permit completion of her cruising programme. *Fairland* (ex-*Carinthia*) and *Fairwinds* (ex-*Sylvania*) are now employed between Europe and Australia under the Liberian flag.

[34] *QUEEN ELIZABETH 2* 1969– Brown

65,850t. 885 × 105 1–1 GT–2 28k.

Laid down on 5 July 1965 and launched 20 Sept. 1967. The contract specified delivery in May 1968, but *Queen Elizabeth 2* did not leave the shipyard until November 1968. Turbine defects caused further postponement and cancellation of a programme which had been promulgated. *Queen Elizabeth 2* finally left Southampton on her maiden New York voyage, 2 May 1969. Information about this ship's inception appears on page 26. Employment is to be cruising from New York for six months a year and this is expected to be rather more profitable than her transatlantic work. Dimensions have been controlled by the need to be able to pass through the Panama and Suez Canals. Overall length is 963 feet. Cost is about £29½ million of which the British Government undertook to lend up to £24 million on very favourable terms, but not quite all of that was required. The builders lost heavily on *Queen Elizabeth 2*'s construction.

Passenger capacity is 564 First Class and 1441 Tourist. Style of the public rooms, cabin furnishings, etc., is essentially modernistic. *Queen Elizabeth 2* is easily the largest and most powerful twin-screw liner ever built. Oil consumption is only half that of *Queen Elizabeth* and S.H.P. 110,000 compared with 150,000. Service-speed is quoted as 28½ knots, but it is unlikely that the extra fuel expenditure will be incurred to make Atlantic crossings at this speed.

Chapter II

Other British Lines

CANADIAN PACIFIC LINE – ANCHOR LINE – DONALDSON LINE – FURNESS WARREN LINE

(For Red Star Line *see* under Bernstein (Red Star) Line, Chapter V.)

CANADIAN PACIFIC LINE (1903–)

FUNNEL – (a) *Buff*
(b) *1947. Buff with house-flag*
(c) *1968. Green (darker shade aft) with white symbol (see* Empress of England *photograph on page 89)*

FLAG – (a) *Six squares, white and red, diced*
(b) *1968. Dark green to hoist, a lighter green to fly, white symbol—*

HULL – *Green waterline for all ships and white hulls for* 'Empresses'. *The* 'Empresses' *also had a blue riband which was exchanged for a green in 1947. In 1968 the riband was expanded into a wide green band and* '*CP Ships*' *painted in black on either side.*

A feature of North American railway expansion was that when rails reached salt-water the company concerned usually took prompt action to ensure that a shipping line carried freight, and preferably also passengers, to and from the new railhead. The Canadian Pacific was among the majority following this practice, although unusual in favouring direct ownership instead of co-operation. Railway-owned liners left for China in 1891, not so long after the first train from Montreal arrived at Vancouver. Ten years later the Canadian Pacific Railway gained the Atlantic at St. John, New Brunswick, and the company's steamship line to the United Kingdom began operations in 1903. The line was not actually a new one, but a purchase from Elder, Dempster & Company. The fleet thus acquired consisted almost entirely of freighters, though many had ample accommodation for emigrants, and the only additions up to August 1914 were two liners of high standard which won for the company a half-share in the mail contract. Two Cabin Class vessels were approaching completion, however, and indicated intent to increase travel facilities for passengers in more affluent circumstances than the average emigrant. The Dominion's oldest and most important shipping concern, the Allan Line, was bought during the war years and the two fleets were combined under the Canadian Pacific house-flag.

The Canadian Pacific Line secured both the cream and the greater part of the Dominion's Western Ocean passenger traffic throughout the inter-war years. Liners built to its own specifications, ex-Allan vessels and two former German ships provided weekly departures for Quebec and Montreal from each of three ports—Liverpool, Glasgow and Southampton. Liverpool had long been the principal starting-point for Canada; the Clyde service was inherited from the Allan Line and the Southampton liners, originally fortnightly, began their voyages from Antwerp. Winter voyages of these Cabin ships were on a reduced schedule and made direct from the United Kingdom to St. John. The world slump of the early 1930's caused the Glasgow service to be dropped and the Liverpool re-routed via Greenock.

About the same time the Antwerp steamers transferred their European terminal to Southampton. *Prima donnas* of the fleet were two luxurious liners which were dignified by '*Empress*' names and carried three passenger classes. After May 1922 they sailed from Southampton to Quebec via Cherbourg over the months the St. Lawrence was ice-free and made long-distance cruises in winter. The 24-knot *Empress of Britain* of 1931 was one of the outstanding ships of this century and fully equal to the best tonnage on the New York route. Unfortunately her running-mate, *Empress of Australia*, lacked the speed to partner her adequately.

Conclusion of World War II found the Canadian Pacific with a sadly-reduced passenger fleet and only the Liverpool service was restored. The two surviving Cabin liners were raised to '*Empress*' status and one of them, *Empress of Canada*, resumed the company's passenger sailings on 16 July 1947. Addition of *Empress of Scotland* from the pre-war transpacific fleet allowed weekly departures from May 1950, although for two years she proceeded no further than Quebec. Extra speed enabled her to call at Greenock, whereas the ex-'*Duchess*es' sailed directly from Liverpool to Canada. Three new ships had replaced *Empress of Scotland* and the slower pair by

1961 in which year the route, Liverpool–Greenock–Quebec–Montreal, became common to all. Winter voyages were to St. John and made only twice every three weeks, because one *Empress* was then withdrawn for cruising. The Canadian Pacific Railway has no track linking Nova Scotia with the main system and consequently its ships have normally omitted the Halifax call of other lines on the winter route. Mail commitments however compelled some modification and between 1931 and 1949 Halifax appeared in the itinerary of mail-carriers on passage to and from St. John.

The Canadian passenger trade boomed during the 1950's and then fell away rapidly. Foreign shipping companies which had joined in to profit from the demand for passages to the Dominion dropped out. The Canadian Pacific discontinued winter transatlantic voyages in favour of pleasure-cruising in 1962 and two years afterwards reduced the number of summer sailings by one-third. The Cunard's final year in the Canadian passenger trade was 1967 and the Holland–America's (one ship only) 1968. Regular passenger departures are now limited to eight months a year and the Canadian Pacific makes two every three weeks. The other participants are the Polish Ocean Lines and the Baltic Steamship Company which each have a Montreal sailing about once a month.

At the end of the 1920's the Canadian Pacific possessed one of the largest Western Ocean passenger fleets, but the subsequent world shipping depression caused many vessels to be laid up and later sold. Among them were *Empress of France* (ex-Allan *Alsatian*), *Metagama*, *Melita* and *Minnedosa* which were not sold until 1934–35 although they saw no active employment in those years. They have therefore been omitted from the following ship-list. Another omission is *Beaverbrae* (ex-German *Huascaren*), a special vessel used between 1948 and 1954 to carry 'Displaced Persons' from Bremerhaven.

The Canadian Pacific fleet has always included cargo ships and one which earned immortality should be mentioned, since by some inexplicable chance her name has escaped general record. *Beaverford* belonged to Halifax Convoy '*HX.84*' which on 5 November 1940 encountered the 'pocket battleship' *Admiral Scheer*. The escorting armed merchant cruiser, *Jervis Bay*, at once attacked, although her swift destruction was a certainty. The convoy scattered and *Admiral Scheer* pursued the nearest large ship, *Beaverford*. The White Ensign was gone and *Beaverford*, though only armed for defence against submarines, must keep her Red flying to the last to allow more fortunate vessels to speed away in other directions. Her fight with the *Admiral Scheer* began about sundown and skill combined with fortune enabled her to resist until nearly an hour before midnight. Then *Beaverford* blew up, leaving no survivors.

The Canadian Pacific employs five North Atlantic freighters which operate between Britain and Great Lakes ports, and three large container ships were ordered in September 1968. Three months earlier the company had adopted a common symbol to cover its many activities and be displayed against colours varying with each operational sphere. The colour allocated to the fleet was green and this brought about a new funnel and house-flag. The ships were redesignated 'C.P. Ships' at the same time.

The company is incorporated in Canada, but the transatlantic 'C.P. Ships' are British-registered and manned.

[41]	*MONTCALM*	1922–39	Brown
[42]	*MONTROSE*	1922–40	Fairfield
[43]	*MONTCLARE*	1922–39	Brown

16,400t. 549 × 70 2–2 GT–2 16k.

Ships of this class were built with 540 Cabin and 1270 Third passenger berths, but much of the Third Class accommodation was altered to Tourist in later years. The second and third ships were at first to have been called *Montmorency* and *Matapedia.* Exchanging their double-reduction for single-reduction geared-turbines in 1929–30 rectified an excessive fuel consumption. The *Montcalm*s began by working from the Mersey, but usually sailed from Southampton after re-engining.

Requisitioning in October, September and August 1939 respectively was for combatant employment as armed merchant cruisers and two received new names to avoid confusion with regular British and French warships. '*U.99*' sank *Forfar* (ex-*Montrose*) west of Ireland on 2 Dec. 1940. The Admiralty converted *Wolfe* (ex-*Montcalm*) and *Montclare* to depotships early in 1942 and bought them outright in May–June that year. *Wolfe* was broken up, 1952; *Montclare*, 1958.

[44] *EMPRESS OF AUSTRALIA* ('19) 1927–39 Stettin

21,850t. 590 × 75 3–2* GT–2 18½k.

A handsome and luxurious liner launched in 1913 as *Tirpitz*, the largest of a trio ordered by the Hamburg–American Line for a new River Plate service (*see Resolute* [195]). They were designed as miniature *Vaterland*s (*see Leviathan* [83]) and the two effective funnels similarly split at main-deck level. *Tirpitz*, however, had novel machinery—turbines with hydraulic transformers conveying the power to the propeller-shafts. An oft repeated story that the German

Emperor ordered completion in 1916 to serve as his yacht is fictitious, the truth being that work was temporarily resumed with a view to fitting out as a naval hospital ship. She was surrendered to Great Britain and bought by the Canadian Pacific, July 1921, for transpacific employment. The new owners named her *Empress of Australia* and altered the coal-fired furnaces to burn oil. Weight of the superstructure made the carriage of 1000 tons of permanent ballast necessary.

In the Pacific the unusual main machinery proved most unsatisfactory. The designed service-speed of 17 knots could not be maintained and fuel consumption was excessive. The liner was therefore brought home and sent to the Fairfield yard for re-engining with single-reduction geared turbines and fitting new boilers. These alterations raised speed to about 18½ knots and cut oil expenditure from 205 tons a day to 150. *Empress of Australia* was re-allocated to the Southampton–Cherbourg–Quebec route with a first voyage, May 1927. Re-engining had been accompanied by conversion of propellers to inward-turning, a change which saved a little fuel but made her a very difficult ship to manoeuvre. By 1933 accommodation had been modified and regraded to give a passenger complement of 387 First Class, 394 Tourist and 358 Third.

Empress of Britain of 1931 became her partner on the Canadian mail service and from that date *Empress of Australia* operated on the tightest of schedules in order to fit in as best she could with the 24-knot newcomer. This left her without any reserve speed. In May 1939 she took the Royal Family to Canada and a much delayed arrival at Quebec became inevitable when she ran into heavy fog. Four months later *Empress of Australia*, last survivor of the ex-German liners under the British flag, was converted to a troop-transport and she continued in this capacity until sold to shipbreakers in 1952.

[45]	*DUCHESS OF BEDFORD*	1928	Brown
	EMPRESS OF FRANCE	1948–60	
[46]	*DUCHESS OF ATHOLL*	1928–42	Beardmore
[47]	*DUCHESS OF RICHMOND*	1929	Brown
	EMPRESS OF CANADA	1947–53	Brown
[48]	*DUCHESS OF YORK*	1929–43	Brown

20,100t. 580 × 75 2–2 GT–2 18k.

Important ships, introducing a higher standard of Cabin Class accommodation which was little inferior to the average First elsewhere. The improvement was so marked that the Canadian Pacific adopted a special style of ship-nomenclature for these four Cabin liners. *Duchess of Bedford* and her sisters could carry 580 travellers in their Cabin Class, 480 in the Tourist and 510 Third. Five ships were ordered, but the fifth was cancelled and her name transferred to the fourth which had been laid down as *Duchess of Cornwall.* The quartette usually worked from Liverpool and often cruised in winter. *Duchess of Atholl* lost her rudder on an October 1935 crossing and arrived in the Mersey three days late.

The '*Duchess*es' made ideal troopships, *Duchess of Bedford* being requisitioned in August 1939 and the others in December 1939, February and March 1940 respectively. Two were lost on the Cape route to Egypt. '*U.178*' sank the northbound *Duchess of Atholl* some 200 miles east of Ascension, 10 Oct. 1942.

Duchess of York and the Anchor *California* [63], proceeding in company to Suez, were destroyed by high-level bombing about 320 miles westward of Oporto on 11 July 1943 with considerable loss of life.

After hostilities the surviving ships of the class were renamed and reconditioned for 400 First and 300 Tourist Class. *Empress of France* was to have been called *Empress of India*, but the name altered on account of India's revised political status. *Empress of Canada* re-opened the passenger service on 16 July 1947. She caught fire alongside her Liverpool dock, 25 Jan. 1953, turned over on her side because of the weight of water poured into her and became a total loss. From April to November 1957 the Canadian Pacific had four passenger ships running between the Mersey and Montreal, and *Empress of France* worked on a schedule of her own.

[49] *EMPRESS OF BRITAIN* 1931–40 Brown

42,350t. 733×98 3–2* GT–4 24k.

A bold experiment and an outstanding ship of the century. The 1931 *Empress of Britain* (452 First, 260 Tourist, 470 Third) represented an attempt to win American patronage from the Middle and Far West. Accommodation was spacious and the finest afloat, and when she entered service in May 1931 only the Norddeutscher Lloyd's *Bremen* and *Europe* could outpace her. Smartest crossing was 4d. 7h. 58m. (25·08 knots) from Rimouski to Cherbourg in 1934. *Empress of Britain* averaged 4d. 13h. 38m. during her first season (nine crossings either way) which was better than any single passage made by the German record-breakers. Americans bound for Chicago and beyond could travel by this ship to Quebec and save many hours on the full journey.

Empress of Britain was the earliest vessel in which suitability for transatlantic work and long-distance pleasure-cruising were considered equally important. Unlike the *Empress*es which had previously been sent on winter cruises, the possibility of profitable employment in the Canadian trade between December and March was non-existent. Length and draught were kept to the minimum consistent with passing through the Panama Canal. This resulted in the ship being built very high out of the water and the funnels given extra height and girth to obtain some sense of balance. Machinery was arranged to allow steaming on two screws when cruising. *Empress of Britain* possessed speed, size and luxury, but certainly not beauty.

The Canadian Pacific's intention to build a sistership had to be abandoned because of the world trade depression of the 1930's and lack of an adequate running-mate limited *Empress of Britain*'s bid for the mid-Continental traffic. Cruising was entirely from New York and usually took the ship right round the world.

Empress of Britain was laid up at Quebec on first arrival there after outbreak of war. She was taken for trooping in late November 1939, but active service proved short. Homeward bound from Egypt via the Cape, this remarkable liner was attacked by a German bomber 75 miles west of the Aran Islands, 26 Oct. 1940, badly damaged and set on fire. The Polish destroyer *Burza* arrived and took the stricken giant in tow, but she succumbed to a torpedo from '*U.32*' two days later.

[50] *BEAVERHILL* ('28) 1941–44 10,050t. 503 × 62 1–2 GT–2 14k.

One of a class of five cargo steamers which included *Beaverford*. In October 1941 *Beaverhill* was fitted with 138 passenger berths as an emergency measure. Wrecked outside St. John, 24 Nov. 1944.

[51] *EMPRESS OF SCOTLAND* ('30) 1950 Fairfield
Ham. Atl. *HANSEATIC* 1958–66
26,300t. 640 × 84 3–2* GT–2 21k.

Began as *Empress of Japan* of her owners' transpacific fleet. A massive profile suggested *Empress of Britain* of the following year, though without the ungainliness. Her career opened with a record Atlantic crossing (Liverpool–Rimouski in 5d. 5h.). *Empress of Japan* returned to Southampton and sailed from there to Hong Kong via Suez.

In the Pacific she established a speed record, May 1935, with 22·16 knots (6d. 8h. 39m.) from Yokohama to Honolulu and 22·37 between Hawaii and Victoria. Towards the end of 1939 *Empress of Japan* commenced her wartime role of troopship and her name was amended to *Empress of Scotland*, October 1942. Release from trooping duties came in 1948. The Canadian Pacific decided to transfer *Empress of Scotland* to their Atlantic fleet. After reconditioning she re-opened her commercial career in May 1950 with 458 First Class berths and 205 Tourist. She began by 'turning round' at Quebec, but made Montreal her Canadian terminal in the 1952 spring. *Empress of Scotland* had more speed than her running mates and this allowed a regular Greenock call (except 1956). Smartest crossing was 4d. 14h. 42m. from Rimouski to Cumbrae in 1950. Winter occupation was the customary long-distance cruising from New York.

The Hamburg Atlantic (now called the German Atlantic) bought *Empress of Scotland* and extensively reconstructed her before placing in the Cuxhaven–New York service, July 1958, under the name *Hanseatic*. Alterations raised gross tonnage to 30,050, gave a speed of around 20 knots and made her a primarily Tourist Class ship (85 First, 1165 Tourist). Removal of the dummy funnel left *Queen Mary* the only surviving 3-funnelled ocean liner. On 7 Sept. 1966 a disastrous fire broke out in the engine-room a few hours before *Hanseatic* was due to sail from New York. The damage was so extensive that the ship had to be towed to Hamburg. On arrival home she was found not worth the cost of repair and so sold for breaking up.

EMPRESS OF AUSTRALIA 1953–56 *See DE GRASSE* [146]
[52] *EMPRESS OF BRITAIN* 1956 Fairfield
Greek *QUEEN ANNA MARIA* 1965–
[53] *EMPRESS OF ENGLAND* 1957– Tyne (Vickers)
25,500t. 600 × 85 1–1 GT–2 20½k.

148 First, 896 Tourist Class. Larger and slightly faster than the *Saxonia*s, their Cunard equivalents. Best passages of each ship between Liverpool and Rimouski averaged over 21 knots in either direction. *Empress of Britain* made

her maiden voyage in April 1956 and her sister 12 months later. The older ship was the company's regular winter cruising-liner until *Empress of Canada* commissioned.

The night of 8 Nov. 1965 *Empress of England* collided with the Norwegian tanker *Lifjord* when leaving Quebec in a snowstorm for Montreal. Serious damage to the liner's bow compelled her to return to Quebec. In October 1963 *Empress of Britain* was chartered for five years to the Travel Savings Association, an organisation offering cruises at popular prices and then partly owned by the Canadian Pacific Company. After six months, however, the Greek Line bought *Empress of Britain* with delivery in January 1965. The buyers made various alterations, raised the number of Tourist Class berths to 1145 and entered her on the Greek register. She was renamed in English, although after the new Queen of the Hellenes. Maiden departure on the Mediterranean–New York route was in March 1965.

[54] *EMPRESS OF CANADA* 1961– Tyne (Vickers)
27,300t. 600 × 87 1–1 GT–2 20k.

A dual-purpose ship, basically similar to the previous pair and with identical machinery. Beam has, however, been increased by 18 inches and some speed reduction is the result. Overall length is 650 feet against 640. *Empress of Canada* (192 First, 856 Tourist) took her initial Canadian sailing on 24 April 1961. The change in accommodation on her immediate predecessors is due to being designed as the Canadian Pacific's principal cruising liner.

ANCHOR LINE (1856–1940)

FUNNEL – *Black*

FLAG – *White, red anchor*

The prevailing theme of Scotland's story since pre-steamship days has been the outward drain of her people and the Anchor carried more Scots overseas than any other line. Main Anchor service was always between Glasgow and New York without likelihood of attracting English traffic, but the outflow of Scottish migrants seemed endless. Paradoxically the Anchor, the most 'regional' of major British transatlantic shipping companies, was also the most 'foreign'. Search for additional emigrant traffic took small Anchor steamships to Italian ports long before other British lines dreamed of entering the Mediterranean and a Genoa–New York service commenced late in the 1860's. The Anchor became a public company, titled Anchor Line (Henderson Brothers), at end of the century and reconstructed the Glasgow–New York fleet, but size of the new ships illustrates the trade's limitations. *Columbia* of 1902 and three later vessels averaged little over 9000 tons compared with the 18,000–24,000 of the Cunard and White Star 'intermediate' steamers from Liverpool.

In November 1911 the Cunard bought control of the Henderson company, although the Anchor Line remained a separate entity with its Clyde–New York, Italy–New York and also a modest Glasgow–India service. The many competitors who had arisen over the years had greatly reduced the share of the Mediterranean emigrant traffic, but this activity continued to be profitable and was an attraction for the Cunard directors. The Cunard had established a passenger service (mainly emigrant) from the head of the Adriatic to New York under contract with the Hungarian Government seven years earlier. Both the Cunard and the Anchor steamers needed replacement to meet sharpening competition and a Mediterranean joint service was planned. Two pairs of large liners were to be built with the Cunard and the Anchor owning one of each. The first pair, completed in 1914–15, were lost by enemy action and building of the second was postponed.

United States immigration restrictions of the early 1920's killed the Mediterranean–New York trades of both companies. The projected joint-service never materialised and the last Anchor steamer was withdrawn in 1922. The Cunard, however, sought to develop the Clyde–New York route by ordering 17,000-ton ships little inferior to the liners built for the Liverpool service. Glasgow was 'out on a limb' without serious prospect of capturing Atlantic traffic which passed through southern British ports, but this appears to have been overlooked. Potentialities of the Scottish route had been very nicely assessed in the pre-Cunard era, but the five Anchor vessels of the 1920's were too many and too large, and a drying-up of the migrant stream to the United States did not help matters. Attempts to persuade Americans to cross the Atlantic for a holiday in Scotland or to enter the United Kingdom through Glasgow proved ineffective. Some mitigation was obtained by using one vessel to augment the Cunard's Cabin service from Southampton and sending one or more to India during the winter. Moville on the Donegal side of Lough Foyle was the Anchor's Irish call of very long standing, but the Partition of Ireland introduced some complications. So from April 1929 Moville was reduced to three calls a month and the fourth made at Belfast. The Anchor Line company was in no condition to survive the World Depression of the 1930's and in May 1935 a court order was made for the compulsory winding up of the firm, Anchor Line (Henderson Brothers). The fleet and other assets were sold to a new company which eventually took the plain name, Anchor Line. Cunard interest in the Anchor ceased and also Anchor in the Donaldson Line.

Demise of the White Star left the Cunard and the Anchor the only two British lines remaining in the New York passenger trade and they clashed in 1936–38. Some Cunard Liverpool–New York voyages were routed via the Clyde. The Anchor retaliated by sending steamers round the south of Ireland and calling at Dublin and Cobh. The 'war' was ended by agreement at the end of 1938. During the late 1930's Anchor passenger earnings on the North Atlantic failed to recover as did those of other companies and the new owners displayed greater interest in the Indian service which they revitalised with much improved ships. A purchaser for the unwanted fifth Atlantic steamer was found in April 1939. Government requisitioning deprived the line of three others in September of the year, leaving only *Cameronia* in commercial service and she was taken for trooping the next year. The Anchor's transatlantic liners were unlucky in war. Only one, the oldest, survived the 1914–18 holocaust and history exactly repeated itself in 1939–45. The Indian trade was further developed after World War II, but the New York passenger service not revived. Western Ocean passenger lists were becoming more and more international and the day of British West Coast ports as Atlantic passenger terminals was drawing to a close. Liverpool, yet alone Glasgow, could no longer compete effectively with Southampton which could be used in conjunction with a French call.

The company retained a small cargo connection across the Atlantic and placed three 'Twelves' on the New York route in 1945–46. Ownership of the Anchor Line changed hands again in 1953 and the 'Twelves' were transferred to the Bombay trade three years later. In 1966 the line had been reduced to a small cargo concern, and the goodwill and other assets were sold.

[61] *CAMERONIA* 1921–40 Beardmore

16,250t. 552 × 70 1–2 GT–2 16k.

Cameronia was the first British passenger liner laid down after the 1914–18 War and construction proceeded so rapidly that she entered the water 9½ months after laying the keel-plate. The Cunard *Lancastria*, ex-*Tyrrhenia* [10], was a sister. Both liners were built by Beardmore and odd units in their respective fleets. In 1914 the Cunard had contracted with Beardmore for their second ship of the Anchor–Cunard Mediterranean joint-service, but work was never started. The cumbersome name, *Tyrrhenia*, obviously belongs to the same series as the joint-service's war losses (*Transylvania* and *Tuscania*) and *Lancastria* must certainly have been a replacement for the unexecuted contract. *Cameronia* doubtless represented a corresponding Anchor contract with the same shipyard. Had she not been intended for the Mediterranean–New York route, the Anchor Line would hardly have ordered four ships for the Glasgow–New York service. General information about *Cameronia* appears under *Transylvania* (below).

Cameronia left New York for the Clyde, 4 Nov. 1940, on what proved to be the Anchor's last Atlantic passenger sailing and was requisitioned for trooping on arrival home. She was heavily damaged by aerial torpedo while in convoy off Algeria, December 1942, but managed to struggle into port. Post-war employment was further trooping and carrying settlers to Australia for the Ministry of Transport who bought the ship in 1951 and re-registered her as *Empire Clyde*. Broken up, 1958.

[62]	*TUSCANIA*	1922	Fairfield
	Greek *NEA HELLAS*	1939	
	Greek *NEW YORK*	1955–61	
[63]	*CALIFORNIA*	1923–43	Stephen

16,900t. 552 × 70 1–2 GT–2 16k.

See Transylvania (below) for the record of this pair as Anchor liners.

The General Steam Navigation of Greece bought *Tuscania*, April 1939, to inaugurate their Piraeus–New York service under the name *Nea Hellas*. Late in 1940 she was taken over as a British troopship and put under Anchor management. *Nea Hellas* reverted to her owners and 1939 route at the beginning of 1947. Early in 1955 her name was altered to *New York* and she replaced *Olympia* in the Bremerhaven–New York service. Accommodation had then become 84 First Class and 1300 Tourist. This ship was unusual among early Greek Line vessels in flying the Greek national ensign. From November 1959 *New York* was laid up at Piraeus.

[64]	*TRANSYLVANIA*	1925–40	Fairfield
[65]	*CALEDONIA*	1925–40	Stephen

17,000t. 552 × 70 3–2* GT–2 16k.

In 1919–20 the Anchor Line ordered five ships for the North Atlantic—*Cameronia* [61] and four to work from the Clyde. Structural differences were small. *Cameronia* had one promenade deck, but the others two. Construction of *Transylvania* and *Caledonia* was suspended for two years and they were finished with a dummy funnel on either side of the real one. *Cameronia* and the two *Tuscania*s began with passenger complements of 265 First, 370 Second and 1150 Third Class; the last two vessels carried 264, 458 and 620.

Completion of the second pair gave the Anchor Line five post-war North Atlantic liners and permitted sale of the veteran *Columbia*, but one of the new ships was still in excess of Glasgow–New York requirements. *Tuscania* was, therefore, converted to Cabin Class and sailed from Southampton under Cunard colours from May to October, though with Anchor personnel. From 1927 until 1937 *California* made winter voyages to Bombay and *Tuscania* did the same from 1931. *Cameronia* and *California* were reduced to Cabin-ship status in 1929 and their Second Class accommodation regraded Tourist. In October 1930 *Transylvania* and *Caledonia* also had their Second re-rated Tourist, but kept the First Class. One of the quintette was usually pleasure-cruising from New York or the Clyde, chartered for trooping, refitting or laid up. *Transylvania* on a cruise grounded near Cherbourg 28 March 1929, and was refloated after a few hours but repairs kept her out of action until June. *Tuscania* saw less North Atlantic employment than the others during the 1930's and the company managed to sell her in 1939.

California, *Transylvania* and *Caledonia* joined the Northern Patrol as armed merchant cruisers in September 1939. *Caledonia*, renamed *Scotstoun*, was sunk by '*U.25*' 80 miles west of Barra, 13 June 1940; *Transylvania* by '*U.56*' 35 miles north-west of Inistrahull on 10 August the same year. *California* was converted to a troopship in mid-1942. She and *Duchess of York* [48] were taking troops to Egypt when attacked by high-level bombers some 320 miles west of Oporto, 11 July 1943. *California* was set on fire and had to be abandoned. An escorting destroyer sank her by torpedo shortly after midnight. *Duchess of York* also perished and the survivors from both ships were landed at Casablanca.

DONALDSON LINE (1905–1966)

FUNNEL – *Black with white band*

FLAG – (*Anchor-Donaldson*). *Donaldson flag at main; Anchor flag at fore*

(*Donaldson Atlantic*). *Donaldson flag flown below a long white pennant bearing a thistle* (*green and red*)

(*Donaldson*). *Red-white-blue tricolour with large blue* '*D*' *on the white*

The Donaldson Line of Glasgow was the only exclusively Scottish concern carrying passengers into the St. Lawrence. It started with sailing-ships in the Plate trade and began making seasonal steamship voyages to Montreal in the 1870's. Within a short space of time the sporadic Canadian sailings gave way to regular with the Donaldson steamers carrying emigrants as well as freight, and activities became pretty evenly divided between the St. Lawrence and Plate Rivers.

Canada's immigration boom of the 1900's brought the northern trade into greater prominence with bigger ships and much improved accommodation. The new era began in 1905 when *Athenia* was modified to carry 50 Saloon passengers in addition to 450 Steerage and the number of Saloon was soon increased. By 1912 four steamers with berths for 200–300 Saloon passengers were maintaining a weekly Glasgow–Canada service. Most sailings were to Quebec and Montreal, but the winter voyages made to St. John via Halifax. During World War I the Canadian liners were transferred to a new company, the Anchor–Donaldson, of which the Anchor and the Donaldson each provided half the capital.

Throughout the 1930's two post-war Anchor-Donaldson liners and a pair of Cunarders operated a Canadian joint service, fortnightly voyages from Glasgow with a Liverpool call alternating with Cunard departures from the Mersey via the Clyde. All ships called at Belfast, outward and homeward. A second organisational change occurred when the Anchor Line went into liquidation. From 1935 the Anchor-Donaldson became a purely Donaldson subsidiary, called the Donaldson Atlantic Line.

One passenger liner was lost by enemy action and the other sold in 1946. The Donaldson fleet was always mainly freighter and in 1948–49 two cargo ships were adapted to carry 55 First Class passengers each. They were transferred to the Donaldson-Atlantic, but reverted to the Donaldson Line proper when the subsidiary company was wound up in March 1954. Over the winter months they worked in other Donaldson trades except between 1955–56 and 1961–62 when they ran to Halifax and St. John. They began by charging a fare a little below First Class in the Cunard *Scythia*s from Liverpool, but by the 1960's the passage rate had become much the same as Tourist Class. The ships were withdrawn at the close of 1966 and the Donaldson Line closed down completely the next year.

[71]	*ATHENIA*	1923–39	Fairfield
[72]	*LETITIA*	1925–39	
	CAPTAIN COOK (0)	1955	

13,450t. 526 × 66 1–2 GT–2 15k.

Athenia and *Letitia* approximated cruiser-sterned versions of *Andania* [7]. Passenger capacity in the 1930's was 314 Cabin Class, 310 Tourist and 682 Third. In 1935 *Letitia* stranded on South Briggs Reef in Belfast Lough during fog and remained fast for two days. *Athenia*, outward bound, was torpedoed and sunk by '*U.30*' 250 miles north-west of Rathlin Island 3 Sept. 1939. The fatality which cost the lives of 112 passengers and crew occurred within a few hours of the British declaration of war on Germany and did much to inflame public opinion against that country. *Letitia* had a varied war career. She was first used as an armed merchant cruiser, then as a trooper and from 1944 as a Canadian hospital ship. The Ministry of Transport purchased her, 1946, for regular trooping as *Empire Brent*. In 1952 she was adapted for carrying migrants to New Zealand and the name changed to *Captain Cook*. Three years afterwards her original owners chartered her for seven Glasgow–Liverpool-Montreal voyages with 950 passenger berths at a Tourist Class fare. This attempt to revive passenger traffic along pre-war lines was unsuccessful. Shipbreakers bought the ex-*Letitia* in 1960.

[73]	*LISMORIA* ('45)	1948–66	8350t. 437 × 62 1–2 GT–1 16k.
[74]	*LAURENTIA* ('45)	1949–66	

Previously *Taos Victory* and *Medina Victory*, built at wartime yards in California. The Donaldson Line bought them in 1947 and 1946 respectively and they each carried 12 passengers prior to conversion to passenger-freighters.

FURNESS WARREN LINE (1913–1961)

FUNNEL – *Red with black top, black band and black base*

FLAG – (a) *On blue, a large white 'F'*

(b) *1951. Blue with black-and-red ball and white 'F'*

Between conclusion of the 1914–18 and 1939–45 Wars many British lines dropped out of the transatlantic passenger trade to the United States of America and only two resumed sailings after the second—the Cunard and the relatively minor, Furness Warren. The Furness Warren steamers followed the Liverpool–Halifax–Boston route of the pioneer Cunarders and added a St. John's (Newfoundland) call.

At the beginning of last century Boston still vied with New York as a trans-ocean port, but was fast losing ground by the time the early Cunard paddlers made it their western terminal. Boston's significance as an alternative entrance into the Union faded away with the opening up of the West. Around 1900 the Massachusetts port staged a sharp revival and Furness, Withy & Company who owned a substantial cargo connection with neighbouring Canada and Newfoundland bought the ailing Warren Line (Liverpool–Boston) in 1912. They started a small Liverpool–St. John's–Halifax passenger service the following year and extended the route to Boston in 1919. Two new steamers were substituted for the original pair in 1925–26 and replaced by namesakes after World War II. The title, Furness Warren Line, was not officially adopted until 1947 although it had long been in common use.

Main purpose of the Furness Warren vessels remained conveyance of freight, but the ships listed below came into the passenger liner category even though they were the smallest built for the Atlantic over many years. For Newfoundland and New England they represented the only direct passenger link with Europe; for Nova Scotia, the only link for 8–9 months each year. Though little advertised and purely of regional consequence, they were well patronised. First Class fare of the 1950's was slightly less than by the Donaldson passenger-freighters and the Tourist about £20 cheaper. Popular though the Furness Warren ships had been, by 1961 air-travel left no room for them on the North Atlantic. They were therefore sold and replaced by motor freighters.

[76]	*NEWFOUNDLAND*	1925–43	Barrow
[77]	*NOVA SCOTIA*	1926–42	

6800t. 406 × 55 1–2 4E–1 14k.

105 First, 80 Third Class. War requisitioning of *Newfoundland* was as a hospital ship; of her sister, for trooping. A torpedo from '*U*.177' sank *Nova Scotia* homeward bound from Egypt with 700 Italian prisoners, some 190 miles from Lourenço Marques on 28 Nov. 1942. Survivors totalled 192 in all. Red Cross markings failed to save *Newfoundland* from destruction by air attack off Salerno with heavy loss of life, 13 Sept. 1943.

[78]	*NOVA SCOTIA*	1947–61	Tyne (Vickers)
[79]	*NEWFOUNDLAND*	1948–61	

7450t. 416 × 61 1–2 GT–2 15k.

Modernised versions of the previous pair, each accommodating 75 First and 80 Tourist Class passengers. From commencement of the 1961–62 winter season they were operated as 'Twelves' for 12 months and then sold to the Dominion Navigation Company for a Melbourne–Yokohama service under the names, *Francis Drake* and *George Anson.*

Chapter III

Lines of the United States of America

UNITED STATES LINES (of 1931) – AMERICAN EXPORT ISBRANDTSEN LINES – BALTIMORE MAIL LINE – AMERICAN SCANTIC LINE – AMERICAN BANNER LINES

UNITED STATES LINES (of 1931) (1931–)

FUNNEL – *Red with narrow blue top and white band*

FLAG – (a) *White with blue eagle and lettering—*
(b) 1938. *As above, but without lettering.*

The present United States Lines have had two predecessors of identical name, although quite separate organisations. The existing Lines came into being through purchase from the United States Shipping Board in 1931 and are best distinguished from the earlier by adding '(of 1931)' to their title, although the date forms no part of the official designation. The actual purchaser was the well-experienced International Mercantile Marine Company, but through a subsidiary which was created for the purpose (the United States Lines Company of Nevada) and not eliminated until December 1934. The 1931 transaction represented the Shipping Board's fourth attempt to establish a transatlantic line under the American flag. The United States Mail Line, the United States Lines of 1921 and the 1929 namesake do not belong to this book, but a continuity running through them renders some account obligatory. All operated a passenger service from New York to North-West Europe, using much the same tonnage. Sailings continued without interruption despite the changes and the funnel has remained unaltered since 1921.

In 1920 the Board found itself in possession of a mixed collection of ex-German passenger liners which had been seized in American ports and a fleet of war-built transports, readily convertible into commercial passenger vessels of a modest type. The United States Mail Line used the Board's ships on charter and collapsed ignominiously, August 1921. The Shipping Board then took over on its own account and altered the name to United States Lines. The main route was New York–Bremerhaven with British and French calls. Financial losses were heavy and the Board anxious to rid itself of the liability. The United States Lines' name, fleet and trade connection were offered for sale and on 21 March 1929 went to P. W. Chapman & Company. A quarter of the purchase price was paid in cash and the balance plus interest payable in instalments spread over 15 years. An important stipulation required the buyers to build two 45,000-ton ships to partner the ex-German *Leviathan*. Sailings of the preceding organisation were continued, though Hamburg was soon substituted for Bremerhaven as the German terminal. Congress had increased the already high mail subsidies in 1928, but such prospects of success as the United States Lines (Chapman) may have possessed were wrecked by the world shipping slump which set in. Instead of the two 45,000-ton vessels the Chapman Company ordered a pair of smaller Cabin Class liners. It also failed to maintain the instalment payments and the United States Shipping Board foreclosed, October 1931. The United States Lines were resold to the International Mercantile Marine Company (generally known as the 'I.M.M.') and the third phase opened. There was, however, a difference from previous occasions of alteration of owner and operator. In 1921 and 1929 the predecessor's entire fleet had been taken over, but only *Leviathan* and two converted troopships were bought by the 'I.M.M.'. The transaction included, however, the Cabin Class liners still under construction and this meant fewer sailings until the latter were ready. Also included were five passenger-freighters which the Chapman company had operated separately as the American Merchant Line. Two similar vessels were added and all seven absorbed into the United States Lines.

The 1931 house-flag resembled that of the American Line of 1893 except that the letters 'USL' were added and this brings out a vital difference between the new United States Lines and the earlier ones. The 'I.M.M.' was an experienced ship-operator. The International Mercantile Marine worked through subsidiaries and in the 1890's already owned the American Line and the Belgian-flag Red Star. The American ships were not replaced as they aged, but

British-flag vessels were added. Use of the Red Ensign as a 'flag of convenience' had many advantages and an enormous expansion occurred in the early 1900's when the Harland & Wolff chairman induced the 'I.M.M.' to buy the British lines for which his company had recently built extensively. The most important was the White Star and a controlling interest was also obtained in the Holland–America. The 'I.M.M.' thus became a gigantic combine with nearly all its tonnage under 'flags of convenience' and the last American-flag vessels had disappeared from the transatlantic fleets by 1922. Shortly afterwards the 'I.M.M.' started disposing of the British lines so that it could take advantage of the inducements which Congress began offering shipowners working under the American ensign and by 1931 was in a position to buy the United States Lines. To complete this aspect of the story, the 'I.M.M.' changed its title to the United States Lines Company in May 1943.

The former American merchant steamers continued on their old route to London and concerned themselves mainly with cargo. Completion of the Cabin Class pair (*Manhattan* and *Washington*) allowed weekly New York–Hamburg passenger sailings from mid-1933. The new liners normally touched at Plymouth (eastbound), Cherbourg and Southampton (westbound); the ex-troopships added Cobh and made Havre their French call. The steady money-loser *Leviathan* which the Shipping Board insisted should remain in operation 'turned round' at Southampton, but at the beginning of 1935 consent was given to lay her up permanently on condition that the United States Lines replaced her with a third Cabin Class liner.

The United States Lines of 1931 established itself on the Western Ocean where others had failed, though the owners' practical experience was only one of several contributory factors. The world trade depression passed and in 1933 repeal of the Volstead Act which had prohibited sale of alcoholic refreshment brought passengers who had hitherto shunned American ships. Even more important was the 1936 Merchant Marine Act which provided that the government should pay the excess cost incurred in building in the United States rather than at a foreign shipyard and lend the shipowner three-quarters of the remainder. Operational subsidies for passenger liners and freighters were also raised.

Neutrality legislation forbade American ships trading with belligerent countries and World War II consequently brought immediate suspension of United States Lines' services to North-

West Europe, although *Manhattan* and *Washington* sailed between New York and Italy as long as this remained permissible. Arrangements had already begun to build a freighter fleet under the 1936 Act and eight of the smaller vessels were therefore transferred to a new 'I.M.M.' creation, the Antwerp Navigation Company, a Belgian subsidiary. Soon afterwards the rest of the 1939 fleet was bought by the government for conversion to troopships.

In 1946 the United States Lines had large cargo fleets working on the North Atlantic and Pacific Oceans, and cargo-carriage has since remained the major activity. American vendors have the right to repurchase their vessels from the government when the emergency has passed, but the United States Lines only exercised the option in the case of the new Cabin Class ship, *America,* which took her maiden commercial sailing for Europe late in 1946. Fifteen months later *Washington* was partly reconditioned and chartered. With only two passenger liners running, the route became New York–Cobh–Havre–Southampton–Hamburg with the newer usually proceeding no further than Southampton. Hamburg was dropped in favour of Bremerhaven and *Washington* relinquished at close of the 1951 season. The record-breaker *United States* commissioned the July following and still remains the fastest Western Ocean liner. She was, however, designed with wartime employment as troopship kept constantly in mind and basic fares are a little less than in corresponding British and French vessels. American operational subsidies normally cease when a ship is over twenty years old, but the period was extended to enable *America* to continue running until 1964. *United States* has since been the only American passenger liner trading to North-West Europe and extends most voyages to Bremerhaven. Occasional calls are made at Cobh.

The United States Lines have expanded their cargo services to the extent that they now own some 50 ships and many of the freighters carry a few passengers. Development of the container-ship has been prominent and six 18,750-ton vesesls of this description (the *American Lancer* class) are in service. The business had, however, been operated at a loss until the possibility of further developing the freight side attracted the attention of Walter Kidde & Company, an industrial 'complex', to which the former International Mercantile Marine sold the United States Lines at the end of 1967.

Gross tonnages recorded in the following fleet-list are either by

European rules or are estimates. Measurement of passenger liners by American rules produces markedly lower figures.

[81] *PRESIDENT ROOSEVELT* ('22) 1931–40 } Camden, N.J.
[82] *PRESIDENT HARDING* ('22) 1931–40 }
14,150t. 516 × 72 1–2 GT–2 18k.

Laid down as army transports, but redesigned as commercial vessels on the stocks. They were completed for the United States Lines (Shipping Board) early in 1922 as *Peninsula State* and *Lone Star State* respectively, renamed *President Pierce* and *President Taft* in May and again renamed *President Roosevelt* and *President Harding* after three months. They looked essentially freighters with four 'goalpost' masts for working cargo and their masts proper were signal-poles mounted on the second and third. Passenger accommodation was altered to 320 Cabin Class and 324 Third in 1924.

These two liners called at Cobh until United States Lines' sailings were suspended in September 1939. In February the next year *President Harding* was transferred to the Antwerp Navigation Company and became the cargo steamer *Ville De Bruges*. German bombers sank her in the Scheldt on 14 May 1940. The United States bought *President Roosevelt* for conversion to the trooper *Joseph T. Duckman* and she lasted until 1948.

[83] *LEVIATHAN* ('14) 1931-37 Hamburg (Blohm & Voss)
54,300t. 907 × 100 3–2* T–4 23½k.

Leviathan was the name given to the German *Vaterland*, the world's biggest ship which had sought sanctuary at New York on her fourth round-voyage and been seized by the United States on 4 April 1917.

Vaterland was the second of three giant liners the Hamburg–American company had ordered shortly before World War I. The first, *Imperator*, became the Cunard *Berengaria* [3]; the last, to have been called *Bismarck*, was completed in 1922 as the White Star *Majestic* [18]. Respective lengths were 883, 907 and 915 feet. Each was specifically designed to be larger than the one before and none ever underwent a refit substantially altering her capacity. British measurements of *Berengaria* and *Majestic* differed little from the German, but two widely divergent gross tonnages claimed for the second ship after she became *Leviathan* were clearly farcical. *Leviathan*'s tonnage shown above is her German measurement as *Vaterland* and there is no practical alternative to its acceptance. General design was the same throughout the trio, but *Leviathan* and *Majestic* possessed more in common than either with the Cunarder. Beam of these two was increased in the light of the *Titanic* disaster and they had the same funnel arrangements. All three had a dummy after-funnel and in the ex-*Imperator* uptakes to the first and second were led through the middle of the ship in conventional manner. In the ex-*Vaterland* and ex-*Bismarck* they were divided to port and starboard, and united just beneath the funnels. *Imperator* required considerable modification after completion and the experience gained brought alterations to the later vessels. *Leviathan* was almost certainly the best of the three.

First employment of *Leviathan* as an American ship was inevitably trooping. In February 1922 she began a drastic overhaul which included alteration of furnaces to oil-firing and reconversion to a passenger liner. Measurement rules were framed which gave a tonnage of 59950 gross and, if taken seriously, meant she was larger than *Majestic*. Despite this nonsense, the reconditioned *Leviathan* was a fine and altogether outstanding liner. She joined the United States Lines (Shipping Board) fleet and left New York on her first American commercial sailing, 4 July 1923. Throughout her subsequent career *Leviathan* was unique among the Lines' ships in making Southampton her European terminal. Her French call was Cherbourg and she usually put into Plymouth eastbound. Best passages were 5d. 8h. 38m. from the Ambrose to Cherbourg (24·81 knots) in 1923 and 24·28 knots westward in 1925.

Through no fault of her own, *Leviathan* consistently proved a 'white elephant' and was frequently laid up. Figures for 1926, a typical year, show that the former *Vaterland* sailed with half her passenger accommodation unoccupied. Basic trouble was lack of a suitable running-mate, but high operational costs and the Volstead (Prohibition) Act were others. Losses averaged around $80,000 a voyage.

Leviathan was the only ex-German liner included in the 1931 sale. The new owners promptly remeasured her and gross tonnage tumbled to 48,950. This saved dock dues, but made her smaller than *Berengaria*! In a further effort to make *Leviathan* profitable, the Second Class accommodation was regraded Tourist and passenger complement became 940 First, 666 Tourist and 1402 Third. The French call was altered from Cherbourg to Havre. Structural weaknesses began to show themselves and she was twice laid up. The new *Washington* commissioned in 1933 and the following year *Leviathan* made five round-voyages to Southampton between June and September, arriving back at New York for the last time on 14 Sept. She was paid off and laid aside until sale in December 1937 for scrapping at Rosyth.

[84]	*AMERICAN MERCHANT* ('20)	1931–40	7450t. 436 × 58 1–2 GT–1 15k.
[85]	*AMERICAN BANKER* ('20)	1931–40	
[86]	*AMERICAN FARMER* ('20)	1931–40	
[87]	*AMERICAN SHIPPER* ('20)	1931–40	
[88]	*AMERICAN TRADER* ('20)	1931–40	

Passenger-freighters berthing 78 travellers at the lowest Tourist Class fare on the Atlantic (£20½). They belonged to a group of ships built at Hog Island, Pa., and known as the 'Hog Island Transports'. Original names were *Aisne*, *Cantigny*, *Ourcq*, *Tours* and *Marne*. The five were adapted for commercial usage by the Shipping Board's American Merchant Line in 1924 and ran directly from New York to London until 1940.

The British cargo steamer *Exeter City* had most of her superstructure swept overboard in terrible weather 600 miles east of Cape Race, 10 Jan. 1933. *American Merchant* rescued surviving members of her crew. In February 1940 the quintette were transferred to the Belgian flag as exclusively freighters. A second change of name made them *Ville De Namur*, *Ville D'Anvers*, *Ville De Liége*, *Ville De Mons* and *Ville De Hasselt* respectively. The former *American Banker* survived to become *Arosa Kulm* 236, but the remainder were sunk by German submarines between June 1940 and April 1941.

[89]	*AMERICAN IMPORTER* ('20)	1931–40	7550t. 436 × 58
[90]	*AMERICAN TRAVELER* ('20)	1931–40	1–2 GT–1 15k.

The former 'Hog Island Transports' *Somme* and *Cambrai*, although not converted until 1931. Three years afterwards the United States Lines moved them from the New York–London to a new service, New York–Liverpool via Cobh eastbound and Glasgow and Belfast in the reverse direction. They were transferred to the Antwerp Navigation Company simultaneously with the five *American Merchants* and re-registered as *Ville De Gand* and *Ville D'Arlon*, to be sunk by torpedo in August and December 1940 respectively.

[91]	*MANHATTAN*	1932–40	
[92]	*WASHINGTON*	1933–40	Camden, N.J.
	WASHINGTON (0)	1948–51	

29,650t. 668 × 86 2–2 GT–2 20k.

Manhattan was the first North Atlantic liner built in the United States for 30 years. She and her sister had been ordered by the United States Lines (Chapman), although not completed until the 'I.M.M.' had taken over the Lines. They entered service, August 1932 and May 1933 respectively. Numbers carried were 580 Cabin, 400 Tourist and 150 Third. The pair were the fastest true Cabin Class liners ever built for the Atlantic and the standard of accommodation very high. From January 1940 until Italian entry into World War II they sailed to Genoa instead of Hamburg. Afterwards varied employment was found for them in American waters. *Manhattan* grounded on the Florida coast, January 1941, and remained fast 22 days.

Manhattan and *Washington* were bought by their government, converted to troopships and renamed *Wakefield* and *Mount Vernon*. In conjunction with the renamed *President Roosevelt* [82] and *America* [101] they embarked the British 18th Division at Halifax for Egypt in November 1941 despite American 'neutrality', but were diverted to Singapore. Later transport work was carrying American troops to Europe and *Wakefield* caught fire in a westbound convoy, 3 Sept. 1942. She was abandoned at one stage, but afterwards brought into Halifax and reconstructed at Boston. *Mount Vernon* emerged unscathed from her war service and both vessels were laid up in the Hudson under their original names. The United States Lines chartered *Washington*, February 1948, for renewed commercial employment. Reconditioning was incomplete and provided 1100 berths in a single class at a fare midway between Tourist and Second. *Washington* was relinquished in October 1951 and rejoined her sister in the Hudson after some further trooping. Both vessels were scrapped in 1964.

[93] *MARINE FLASHER* ('45) (0) 1946–49
[94] *MARINE PERCH* ('45) (0) 1946–48
[95] *MARINE MARLIN* ('45) (0) 1946–48
[96] *ERNIE PYLE* ('45) (0) 1946–47
[97] *MARINE FALCON* ('45) (0) 1947–48
[98] *MARINE JUMPER* ('45) (0) 1947–48
[99] *MARINE TIGER* ('45) (0) 1947–49
[100] *MARINE SHARK* ('45) (0) 1947–49

12,500t. 497 × 72 1–2 GT–1 16k.

Troopships under United States Lines' management which carried commercial transatlantic passengers under various arrangements with the Maritime Commission. *Ernie Pyle* derived her name from a popular press correspondent who was killed near Okinawa, April 1945. Main machinery of these ships was right aft. Conditions for their 550 passengers were very austere and the majority slept in 'dormitories'.

[101] *AMERICA* ('40) 1946–64 Newport News

33,550t. 664 × 93 2–2* GT–2 23k.

Built under the 1936 Mercantile Marine Act. *America* was unusual in the fore-funnel being the dummy. She was not completed until June 1940 and began with pleasure-cruises to the Caribbean and California. In July 1941 she was bought for conversion to the troop transport *West Point*. War service resembled that of *Washington* (above). On release *America* was reconditioned to carry 516 First, 371 Second and 159 Tourist Class passengers.

Maiden commercial voyage to Europe started on 14 Nov. 1946 and *America* made an Ambrose–Cobh crossing in 4d. 22h. 22m. (24·4 knots). Size and speed put her into the same category as the Cunard *Mauretania* [24]. An additional 15 feet was added to the height of both funnels during her career. The Second Class was eliminated in 1961 and Tourist accommodation raised to 532. *America*'s last departure for Bremerhaven was from New York on 9 Oct. 1964. She was sold to Chandris Lines and now works between Europe and Australia under the name *Australis* and the Greek flag.

[102] *UNITED STATES* 1952– Newport News

53,350t. 905 × 101 2–1 GT–4 32½k.

The world's fastest ocean liner by a comfortable margin and it is most improbable that a speedier ship of this type will ever be built. Power is much the same as *Queen Elizabeth*, but has been put into a smaller and more elongated hull. Speed is more than enough to make her the 'Blue Riband' holder of the Atlantic and exceeds commercial requirements. *United States* is perhaps best described as a liner-troopship. She was built to the order and specifications of the United States Navy with wartime employment as a troop transport as a primary consideration, but intended for sale to the United States Lines on completion. It was essential that she should be able to pass through the Panama Canal and this consideration controlled her dimensions.

United States was laid down in dry-dock on 8 Feb. 1950, named and floated on 23 June 1951. She cost nearly $77 million to build and the United States Lines paid $33 million. Defence features include watertight sub-division on the same scale as a warship and abnormal fuel stowage. Main machinery is divided between two separate compartments so that *United States* can maintain 20 knots with either engine-room out of action. The ship is absolutely fireproof, woodwork having been eliminated from hull, equipment and fittings, and aluminium has replaced steel wherever practicable in order to save weight. Troop capacity is for 14,000 men.

Maiden voyage to Havre and Southampton commenced, 3 July 1952, and *United States* at once beat *Queen Mary*'s records by 3½–4 knots in either direction. The eastward passage to Bishop Rock occupied 3d. 10h. 40m. (35·59 knots) and the westward 3d. 12h. 12m. (34·51). Accommodation of the highest standard provided for 882 First, 525 Second and 551 Tourist Class, but the First has since been reduced to 675. *United States* averaged 30·63 knots on the 134 passages of her first three years' service. In 1954 she crossed to the Bishop Rock at 32·43 knots and made the same passage two years later in 3d. 17h. 11m. (33·06). Of recent years she has made two or three short cruises every winter. Withdrawal of *Queen Elizabeth* left *United States* the only 3-Class transatlantic liner outside the Mediterranean.

AMERICAN EXPORT ISBRANDTSEN LINES (1931–)

FUNNEL – (a) *Black with broad white band edged with red; on the band, a large blue 'E'.*

(b) Independence, Constitution *and* Atlantic *only until 1962, when adopted for all ships. Buff with narrow blue top and broad white band edged with red.*

FLAG – (a) *On red, a blue 'E' in a large vertical white diamond.*

(b) 1962. *On red, a blue 'E' on a white globe outlined in blue.*

(c) 1964. *Burgee—Upper canton in hoist, blue with white star; cross, red; remainder, white. Rest of flag—blue with white globe (red markings) and blue 'E' superimposed—*

HULL – Independence *and* Constitution *were painted white in 1950, and* Atlantic *on acquisition.*

American Export Isbrandtsen Lines of New York, known simply as the American Export Lines until 1962, has provided the American-flag Mediterranean passenger service. Unlike the United States Lines they began as an exclusively cargo concern, and nearly all

ROTTERDAM [151]

AQUITANIA [2]

STAVANGERFJORD [312]

LACONIA [6]

CALIFORNIA [63]

VEENDAM [153]

DEUTSCHLAND [192]

BERLIN [183]

TRANSYLVANIA [64]

LETITIA [72]

ILE DE FRANCE [142]

EMPRESS OF AUSTRALIA [44]

DUCHESS OF ATHOLL [46]

MILWAUKEE [198]

STATENDAM [154]

BREMEN [185]

EMPRESS OF BRITAIN [49]

LEVIATHAN [83]

PRESIDENT ROOSEVELT [81]

EXCALIBUR [106]

CHAMPLAIN [144]

MANHATTAN [91]

VULCANIA [244]

CONTE DE SAVOIA [246]

GEORGIC [22]

NORMANDIE [145]

PENNLAND [207]

BATORY [332]

QUEEN MARY [23]

NIEWE AMSTERDAM [159]

MAURETANIA [24]

QUEEN ELIZABETH [25]

AMERICA [101]

NOVA SCOTIA [78]

LAURENTIA [74]

LIBERTE [186]

INDEPENDENCE [115]

WATERMAN [173]

UNITED STATES [102]

OLYMPIA [224]

CRISTOFORO COLOMBO [249]

AROSA SUN [238]

CARINTHIA [32]

BERGENSFJORD [315]

EMPRESS OF BRITAIN [49]

EMPRESS OF ENGLAND [53]

STATENDAM [166]

ARKADIA [226]

ATLANTIC [131]

HANSEATIC [51]

BREMEN [187]

ROTTERDAM [167]

EMPRESS OF CANADA [54]

FRANCE [148]

CARMANIA [29]

PRINSES MARGRIET [178]

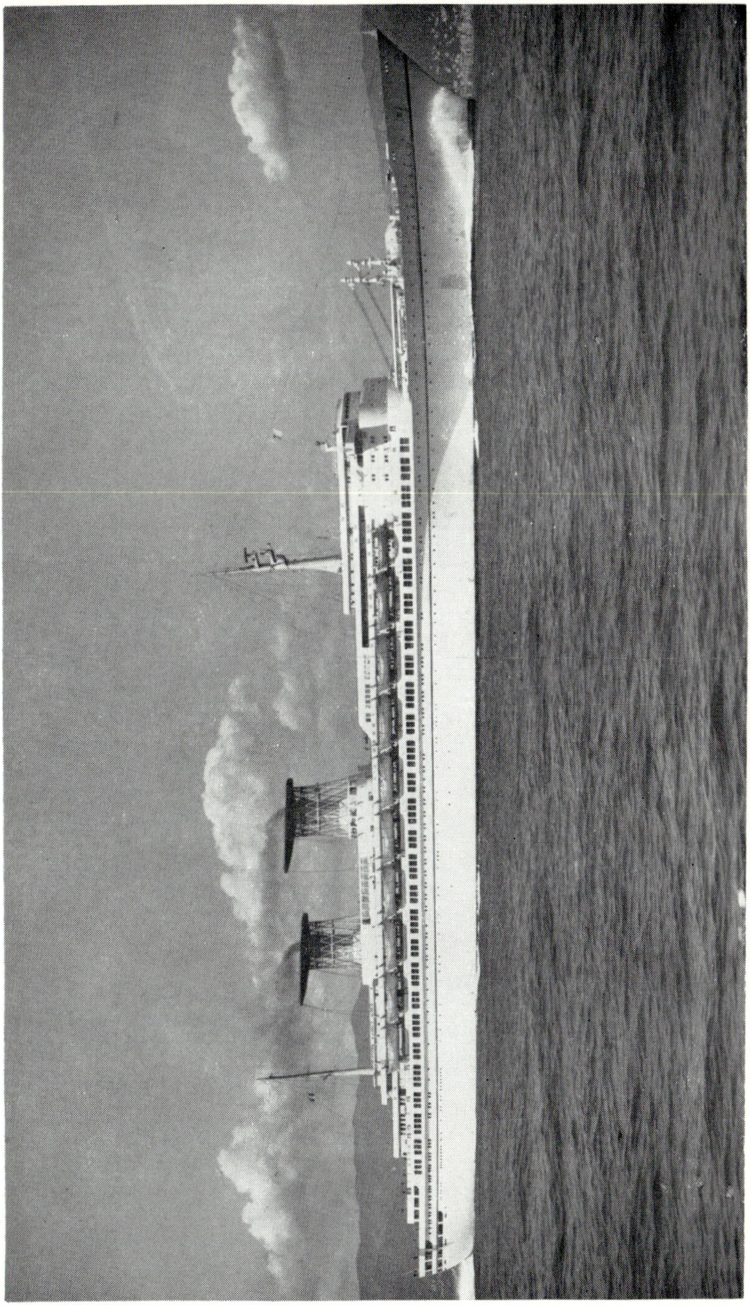

RAFFAELO [254]

SHALOM [304]

ALEXANDR PUSHKIN [336]

KUNGSHOLM [329]

AMERIKANIS [276]

QUEEN ELIZABETH 2 [34]

1

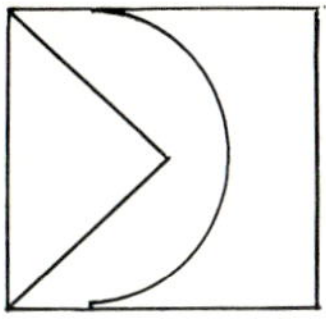

2

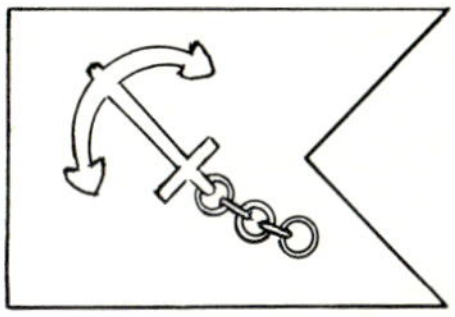

3

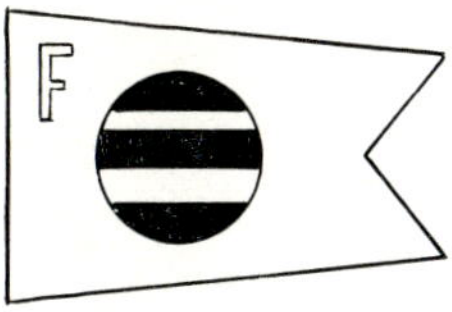

4

5

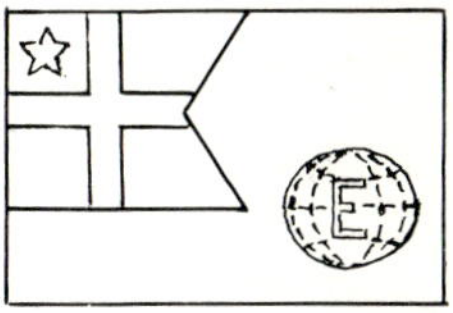

6

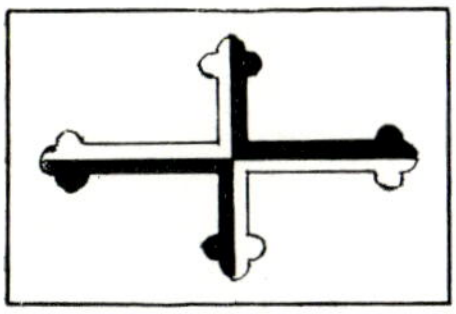

7

8

9

10

11

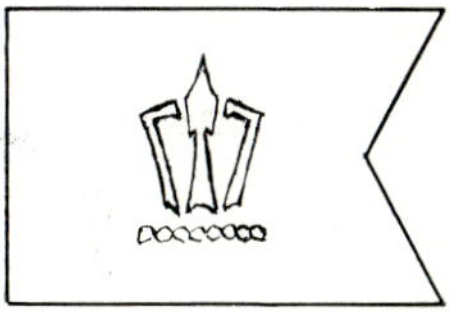

12

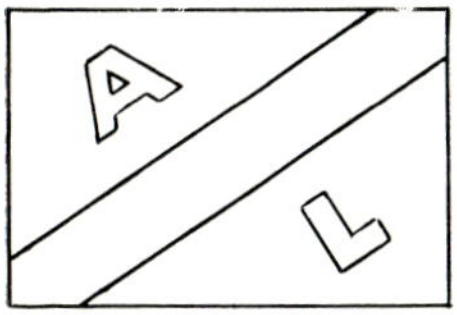

13

14

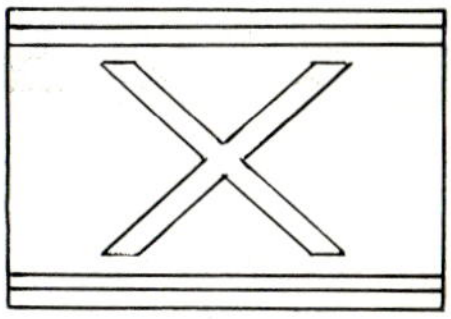

15

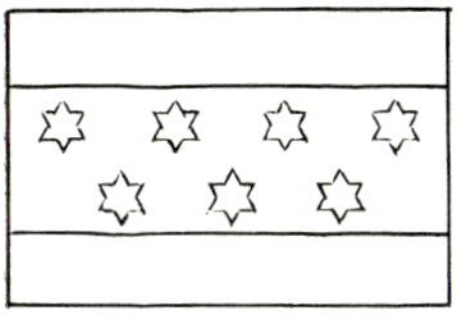

16

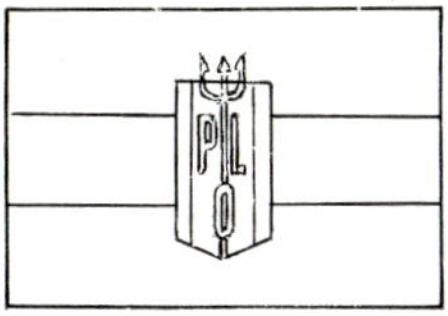

17

18

HOUSE FLAGS

1. Cunard Line:—Red with gold badge.
2. Canadian Pacific Line:—Dark green to hoist, lighter green to fly, white symbol.
3. Anchor Line:—White, red anchor.
4. Furness Warren Line:—Blue, with black and red ball, white 'F'.
5. United States Lines:—White with blue eagle and lettering.
6. American Export (Isbrandtsen) Lines:—Burgee, upper canton in hoist, blue with white star, cross red, remainder white. Rest of flag blue with white globe (red markings) and blue 'E' superimposed.
7. Baltimore Mail Line:—White, particoloured cross, orange and black.
8. Oranje Lijn:—Orange with blue lozenge and white monogram.
9. Norddeutscher Lloyd:—White, blue anchor and key design.
10. Hamburg American Line:—Quartered diagonally, white (top and bottom) and blue, shield yellow, anchor and lettering black.
11. Bernstein Line:—Black and red, white diamond, black letters.
12. Greek Line:—Blue, yellow device with ropework base of pale blue and yellow.
13. Arosa Line:—Blue, with white stripe and letters.
14. Italia Line:—Red cross on white, white fleur-de-lys on red.
15. Chandris Lines:—Light blue, white stripes and letter.
16. Zim Lines:—White, light blue stripes and gold stars.
17. Polish Ocean Lines:—White with red stripe, white and red device.
18. Baltic Steamship Company:—Red, hammer-and-sickle and star yellow.

their fleet still consists of freighters. The year of origin was 1919 and four cargo-passenger liners with good First Class accommodation joined the American Export fleet in 1931. Their normal round-voyage was New York – Marseilles – Naples – Alexandria – Jaffa – Haifa – Beirut – Haifa – Alexandria – Piraeus – Naples – Livorno – Genoa – Marseilles – Boston – New York and lasted 46 days. Three continued a service until 1941. Namesakes of this quartette resumed American Export passenger-freighter sailings in September 1948 and were similarly nicknamed 'The Four Aces'. In principle they worked to the same itinerary as their predecessors, though some modifications crept in. Barcelona was added and later Cadiz. Arab ports refused to handle ships which visited Israel and the American Export steamers then omitted Palestine and called at Latakia and Iskenderun instead for some years. Two 'Aces' were withdrawn in 1959 and the second pair at the beginning of 1965. The place of these passenger-freighters on the Mediterranean 'circuit' has now been taken by 'Twelves'.

Aspirations of the American Export Lines after World War II reached beyond the 'Four Aces'. The only true passenger liners operating on the Mediterranean–New York route in 1948 were an Italian pair of the 1920's and none were under construction. This gave the Export Lines an opening and advantage was taken of the 1936 Merchant Marine Act to order two fast high-grade ships. A chartered vessel which opened a New York–Italy passenger service in 1949 was replaced two years later by the new *Independence* and *Constitution.* They carried three Classes of passenger and after some brief experimenting made their route New York–Gibraltar-Cannes–Genoa–Naples. In 1956 Gibraltar was dropped in favour of Algeciras which had obvious advantages for Spanish passengers and arrangements were made for special trains from Madrid to meet the American Export ships. Withdrawal of two 'Aces' was largely explained by acquisition of the almost exclusively Tourist Class *Atlantic* for an Eastern Mediterranean service (New York–Algeciras–Naples–Messina–Piraeus–Haifa).

Revival of the Italia Line hit the passenger liners hard despite the operational subsidy received for every voyage and the Isbrandtsen Company of New York bought control of the American Export. Isbrandtsen already owned a large cargo fleet and in October 1962 the old and the new interests were amalgamated to form the American Export Isbrandtsen Lines. *Independence* and *Constitution* sought to attract bookings by adding intermediate ports to their itineraries. Among these were Casablanca, Lisbon, Barcelona, Palma and Alghero, but routeing constantly underwent changes. *Atlantic*, too, made Naples her eastern terminal and followed much the same routes as the larger pair. Pleasure-cruising became more and more prominent in the schedules. *Atlantic* which had almost dropped out of transatlantic work altogether was paid off in the 1967 autumn and the Diners-Fugazy Sales Corporation of New York assumed operational control of the *Independence* sisters. Extensive and costly modernising was planned, but only carried out in one ship. Financial losses continued. The 1969 sailings which had been announced were cancelled and both vessels had been laid up by the end of 1968. The future of the passenger side of the American Export Isbrandtsen Lines' business is uncertain.

[106]	*EXCALIBUR*	1931–41	9350t. 450 × 62 1–2 GT–1 16k.
[107]	*EXOCHORDA*	1931–40	
[108]	*EXETER*	1931–41	
[109]	*EXCAMBION*	1931–41	

125 First, later increased to 147. Built at Camden, N.J. *Exochorda* became the transport *Harry Lee*, October 1940, and the Turkish *Tarsus* in 1946, to be burned out in 1960. Her sisters were requisitioned for trooping in 1941. *Joseph Hughes* (*Excalibur*) and *Edward Rutledge* (*Exeter*) fell victims to submarines north of Casablanca on 11 and 12 Nov. 1942. Japanese bombers sank *John Penn* (*Excambion*) off Guadalcanal, 13 August 1943.

[110]	*EXCALIBUR* ('45)	1948–65	9650t. 450 × 66 1–2 GT–1 16½k.
[111[	*EXOCHORDA* ('44)	1948–59	
[112]	*EXETER* ('45)	1948–65	
[113]	*EXCAMBION* ('44)	1948–59	

124 First Class. Ex-troopships *Dauphin, Dutchess, Shelby* and *Queens*, built at Sparrows Point, Md. All took their maiden American Export sailings between September and December 1948. Two were exchanged with the Maritime Commission in part-payment for new freighters. *Excambion* has since been stationed at Galveston and renamed *Texas Clipper*. *Excalibur* and *Exeter* now belong to the Orient Overseas Line (Liberian flag) and are called *Oriental Jade* and *Oriental Pearl*, working between California and Formosa.

[114] *LAGUARDIA* ('44) (0) 1949–51 Kearny, N.J.
c. 18,500t. 573 × 75 2–2 GT–2 20k.

Originally the troopship *General Wilds P. Richardson*, but chartered, refitted to carry 157 First and 452 Tourist Class passengers, and renamed after a Mayor of New York. Gross tonnage by American measurement was 17,950. *Laguardia* ran for American Export Lines from May 1949 till December 1951 and finished with some voyages to Haifa. She was subsequently sold to the Hawaiian Steamship Company who called her *Leilani*, but has been the American President Lines' *President Roosevelt* since 1960.

[115]	*INDEPENDENCE*	1951–	Quincy, Mass.
[116]	*CONSTITUTION*	1951–	

29,500t. 633 × 89 2–1 GT–2 23k.

295 First, 375 Second, 330 Tourist Class. These liners derived their names from frigates which fought successful actions in the War of 1812. Countersterns and two tall funnels of modest girth suggest pre–1914 coal-burners, but are deceptive. Design allows rapid conversion to troopships and *Independence* exceeded 26 knots on trials. *Constitution* began her career with a 5½-day New York–Gibraltar crossing in June 1951, although normal passage time was around 6 days.

Alterations to the superstructure added 110 First Class berths in 1959. Returning to New York after this refit *Constitution* rammed the Norwegian tanker *Jalanta* near the Ambrose Light, 1 March. She cut so deeply into *Jalanta*'s bow that the severed portion afterwards broke right off. *Independence* took her initial 1968 departure for Naples in June after being elaborately redecorated and refitted. Hull and funnels had been repainted in truly remarkable fashion which was explained as designed to 'appeal to the psychedelic generation' (*see* illustration on page 84). Unfortunately it failed to appeal either to the psychedelic or any other generation and in November *Independence* reappeared in orthodox American Export colours. *Constitution* had already been laid up at Baltimore and very soon afterwards the New York dock strike provided a pretext for cancelling the Christmas cruise of *Independence* and sending her to Jacksonville, Florida, for lay-up. It seems unlikely that the American Export Isbrandtsen Lines will employ either these ships or *Atlantic* again.

ATLANTIC 1960– *See* No. 131

BALTIMORE MAIL LINE (1931–1938)

FUNNEL – *Buff with narrow black top and black ring below*

FLAG – *White; parti-coloured cross, orange and black*

The Baltimore Mail Steamship Company was a subsidiary of the 'I.M.M.' (*see* United States Lines) incorporated in 1930. The fleet comprised five former army storeships which the company much improved and fitted out as passenger-freighters. Baltimore

Mail sailings from Baltimore to Hamburg via Southampton and Havre began on 2 July 1931 and a London call was added four years later. The government subsidy was withdrawn in the spring of 1938 on the grounds that the service was unnecessary and the ships were then transferred to another 'I.M.M.' subsidiary, the Panama Pacific Line, for the New York–San Francisco trade.

[121]	*CITY OF BALTIMORE* ('19)	1931–38	8400t. 486 × 56 1–2 GT–1 15½k
[122]	*CITY OF NORFOLK* ('18)	1931–38	
[123]	*CITY OF NEWPORT NEWS* ('19)	1931–38	
[124]	*CITY OF HAMBURG* ('19)	1931–38	
[125]	*CITY OF HAVRE* ('18)	1931–38	

Built as *Steadfast, Independence, Archer, Eclipse* and *Victorious* at Alameda, Cal. Original tonnage was 7600 and turbo-electric machinery propelled these ships at 11 knots. The Baltimore Mail added 46 feet to their length and re-engined them with geared turbines. The passenger accommodation installed provided for 80 Tourist Class. The fourth and fifth vessels were renamed *City of Los Angeles* and *City of San Francisco* on transfer to the Panama Mail. All became World War II troopships and four survived. *William P. Biddle* (ex-*City of Havre*) was sunk by Japanese aircraft off Guadalcanal, August 1942.

AMERICAN SCANTIC LINE (1932–1939)

FUNNEL – *Buff with black top and wide green band bearing a large red 'M' superimposed on a white ball.*

FLAG – *On green, the red 'M' and white ball of the funnel.*

Moore-McCormack Lines started in 1913 with the despatch of a cargo steamer from New York down the east coast of South America, which continent remains the main sphere of operations. The company entered the Scandinavian trade half a decade afterwards and later extended activities into the Baltic. The American Scantic Line was bought from the United States Shipping Board in 1927, but confined to cargo until 1932 when four of the fleet received passenger berths and new names. The route followed was generally New York – Gothenburg – Copenhagen – Gdynia – Stockholm – Helsinki – Copenhagen – New York. Outbreak of World War II brought the sailings to an end.

Resumption of cargo services came in 1945, but American

Scantic passenger facilities are now restricted to 'Twelves' proceeding to Antwerp, Rotterdam, Oslo, Gothenburg and Copenhagen.

[126]	*SCANMAIL* ('19)	1932–39	5150t. 390 × 54 1–2 GT–1 13k.
[127]	*SCANPENN* ('19)	1932–39	
[128]	*SCANYORK* ('19)	1932–39	
[129]	*SCANSTATES* ('19)	1932–39	

Shipping Board cargo steamers, built at Hog Island, Pa., and named *Chickasaw*, *Bird City*, *Schenectady* and *Saguache* until 1932, when equipped with 90 passenger berths at approximately Tourist Class fare. The Brazilian Lloyd purchased the quartette eight years later. Only the last two (renamed *Maua* and *Cantuaria*) survived hostilities.

AMERICAN BANNER LINES (1958–1959)

FLAG – *Flag was identical with the Bernstein Line (see page 99), except that the black was altered to blue.*

FUNNEL – *Funnel was also to have been identical with the Bernstein Line except that the black was changed to blue throughout, but most of* Atlantic's *funnel was repainted white at the last moment to give the house-flag greater prominence. A narrow blue top was left and also a blue strip down to the base so that the funnel looked entirely blue when viewed from right aft.*

The American Banner Lines represented a second attempt by Arnold Bernstein to re-enter the North Atlantic trade (*see* Incres Line, page 147) and the initials on the flag could be interpreted as standing either for 'Arnold Bernstein' or 'American Banner'. Weekly sailings were projected, to be maintained by three ships bought from the United States Maritime Commission and refitted to cater mainly for Tourist Class travellers. The American Government paid the usual subsidy awarded to operators of fast liners, but banned a Southampton call because this would have entailed direct competition with the United States Lines. The route adopted was therefore New York–Zeebrugge–Amsterdam.

The American Banner began with a single ship and *Atlantic* first left New York on 11 June 1958 after three weeks' postponement. Earnings proved inadequate and the two further ships did not materialise. A renewed request to include Southampton in the itinerary was rejected. The American Banner Lines therefore closed down and *Atlantic* left Amsterdam for the last time on 25 October 1959.

[131] *ATLANTIC* ('53) 1958 Chester, Pa.
Am. Export *ATLANTIC* 1960–
18,100t. 529 × 76 1–1 GT–1 20k.

40 First Class, 860 Tourist. Originally called *Badger Mariner*, a cargo steamer built for the Maritime Commission who helped finance conversion. Reconstruction was very extensive and much ingenuity displayed in packing so many passengers into the hull.

The American Export Lines bought *Atlantic* and in May 1960 she started running between New York and Haifa. After two years she proceeded no further than Naples. Passenger complement was reduced to 840 in 1965 and *Atlantic* then became a One Class ship, charging a fare midway between Second and Tourist. Later employment was almost entirely cruising and *Atlantic* laid up at New York on conclusion of her 1967 programme.

Chapter IV

French and Dutch Lines

COMPAGNIE GÉNÉRALE TRANSATLANTIQUE – HOLLAND-AMERICA LINE – NETHERLANDS GOVERNMENT and TRANSOCEAN STEAMSHIP COMPANY – ORANJE LINE

COMPAGNIE GÉNÉRALE TRANSATLANTIQUE
(1864–) *French*

FUNNEL – *Red with black top*

FLAG – *White with red ball followed by red lettering 'Cie Gle' and 'Transatlantique' below*

" 'Bon voyage' is always French" has been the Compagnie Générale Transatlantique slogan of the 1950's and 1960's; 'You are in France the Moment you cross the Gangplank' was its equivalent in the 1930's. The Western Ocean passenger trade is international in clientele and the style of accommodation, cuisine, etc., offered by the major lines so very similar that the nationality of any particular ship is not immediately obvious below the upper-deck. The Cie. Gle. Transatlantique differs, however, from other companies, cultivates a French 'atmosphere' and likens its vessels to the best hotels in France. The French Line, as it has come of recent years to be called in English-speaking countries, has indeed always been something of 'a line apart', competing only indirectly until 1922 when a Plymouth call was established. Route of the Transatlantique steamers had previously (save for a brief interlude in the 1870's) been direct between France and New York, although British, German and American liners embarked and landed passengers on either side of the English Channel. Cunard and White Star, Norddeutscher Lloyd and Hamburg–America, had struggled for the distinction of owning the largest and fastest liners, but the Cie. Gle. Transatlantique remained satisfied with smaller ships of good, although not outstanding, speed. Not until 1935, two years after Italy, could France claim a North Atlantic record-breaker.

Appeal of the French vessels has been centred on 'elegance' and a comparison of *Normandie* with the Cunard *Queen Mary* brings this out strongly. The general post-war trend of paying increased attention to the Tourist Class passenger has reduced the distinctive character, but wine ('vin ordinaire', red and white) continues to be supplied at lunch and dinner.

The Cie. Gle. Transatlantique began operations over a century ago following award of a mail-carriage contract to New York and also to Mexico and the Caribbean. Both routes were originally considered equally important but the southern soon became very secondary to the New York. Links between the company and the French Government have remained close and the succession of contracts granting subsidies have also imposed a measure of control.

The 23,650-ton, 23-knot, *France* which commissioned in 1912, was the first ship this century to be really comparable with the premier British and German liners. *Paris* of 1921 and *Ile De France* of 1927 were substantial improvements and the trio maintained the Havre–Plymouth–New York mail service between them until 1932. Cabin Class ships found favour as the best 'intermediate' type and three were built for the same route. Several North Atlantic companies have used Plymouth for eastbound ships at one time or another, but it has never been popular as an embarkation port and the French Line changed the westward call to Southampton in January 1935.

1935 was the year of the *Normandie*, the most luxurious of Atlantic liners and unique among record-breakers in being propelled by turbo-electric machinery. The orthodox *Queen Mary* which began her career 12 months later equalled *Normandie*'s size and speed. *Normandie* was unfortunate in having slower running-mates than *Queen Mary* and, because they were newer, no immediate provision was made for their replacement. In 1938–39 the French company had the misfortune to lose two New York liners and made arrangements to lay down an enlarged *Normandie* in 1940, but plans failed to materialise for obvious reasons. The Transatlantique service frankly became rather ragged, the ships employed in August 1939 being *Normandie*, *Ile De France*, an excellent Cabin Class ship and a second which was restored to the North Atlantic after some years' absence.

Of the four liners mentioned only *Ile De France* remained afloat in 1945. She had been trooping since 1940 and nine years elapsed before she resumed regular Havre–New York commercial sailings. The scuttled *De Grasse* was raised, reconstructed and put back into North Atlantic work, July 1947. By 1953 the Cie. Gle. Transatlantique had restored a three-ship passenger service to New York with sailings on an approximately weekly basis although unevenly spaced. Financial help from the French Government permitted the laying-down in 1956 of *France*, the largest passenger liner ordered by any company since *Queen Elizabeth* and little inferior in speed to the liner-troopship *United States*. The new *France* commissioned in 1962 and with her advent the French Line adopted Southampton as their homeward British call as well as the outward.

France leaves Havre at fortnightly intervals and is her owners' only passenger vessel running to New York. The French was the first major line to reduce New York passenger sailings to one a fortnight, but the United States Lines followed suit in 1965 and the Cunard in 1968. The Cie. Gle. Transatlantique owns one other ocean passenger liner and employs her in the Caribbean trade. A large cargo fleet includes 19 'Twelves' working on routes to Vancouver, Valparaiso and the West Indies, and the company belongs to the Atlantic Container Lines consortium. The contract with the French Government also covers mail services to Corsica and from Marseilles to Algeria and Tunisia.

[141] *PARIS* 1921–39 St. Nazaire

34,550t. 735 × 85 3–2 T–4 21½k.

Large size and excellent speed, though neither outstanding, made *Paris* a liner of which no other company possessed an equivalent. She had been laid down in 1913, but work twice suspended and the incomplete hull lay in Quiberon Bay for 2½ years. The long delay in construction resulted in her being given oil-fired furnaces instead of coal. Few liners have proved better investments and *Paris* crossed the Atlantic year after year with a lower percentage of vacant berths than any other ship.

Paris, westbound, grounded in fog off the Eddystone on 8 April 1929 and had to return home for repair. That August a fire at Havre demolished much of the accommodation and necessitated a five months' refit. Reconstruction left her passenger complement 560 First, 530 Second and 844 Third. *Paris* caught fire a second time while lying at her Havre berth, 19 April 1939 and the following day heeled over and sank. Outbreak of war prohibited salvage although she was barely submerged.

[142] *ILE DE FRANCE* 1927–58 St. Nazaire

43,150t. 764 × 92 3–2 T–4 23k.

An enlarged and faster *Paris* with a similar profile. Direct-action turbine machinery was retained, although geared had received general acceptance elsewhere. The name painted on her bow was *Ile-De-France*, although the unhyphenated form used for all other purposes. *Ile De France* dispelled the general belief of the early 1920's that the day of the fast liner had passed. She was the earliest of post-1914 design to exceed 19 knots and made one or two crossings at 23½. The standard of accommodation for her 670 First, 408 Second and 580 Third Class was remarkable and even the Third had beds instead of bunks. *Ile De France* was described as the world's most magnificently decorated ship and for some years carried more First Class passengers across the Atlantic than any other liner.

Ile De France was requisitioned after a crossing ex-New York, 1 May 1940, and sent to the Far East. The British took possession of the ship at Singapore in July. Many of her officers assisted in the seizure and she trooped in various theatres with a mixed French and British crew. *Ile De France* reverted to the French flag, September 1945, made one or two commercial New York voyages 12 months later under troopship conditions and then carried French troops to Vietnam.

Re-entry into the Havre–New York service occurred 21 July 1949. Lengthy reconditioning including re-boilering, altering the funnels to two and fitting accommodation for 541 First Class, 577 Cabin and 227 Tourist passengers. In September 1953 *Ile De France* saved the crew of the Liberian freighter *Greenville* in an Atlantic gale. *See* under *Andrea Doria* [348] for the part played in rescue work from that ship, July 1956. *Ile De France* was eastbound 45 miles from the stricken Italian liner, reversed course, embarked 753 survivors and landed them at New York. The following February *Ile De France* grounded when leaving Fort de France on a pleasure-cruise and had to be towed to Newport News for repairs. Final passage from New York to Havre was in November 1958.

[143] *LAFAYETTE* 1930–38 St. Nazaire

25,200t. 577 × 78 1–1 M–4 17½k.

639 Cabin Class, 432 Tourist and 108 Third. The motorship *Lafayette* corresponded with the White Star *Britannic* [21], but the numbers carried in the different classes showed the Cie. Gle. Transatlantique policy of attracting the more affluent passenger. *Lafayette* was almost destroyed by fire in a Havre dry-dock, 4–5 May 1938, and the hull sold to Rotterdam shipbreakers.

[144] *CHAMPLAIN* 1932–40 St. Nazaire

28,100t. 607 × 83 1–2 GT–2 19½k.

Champlain (548 Cabin, 318 Tourist, 134 Third) was an enlarged and steam-driven version of *Lafayette*. The low ratio of beams to length made both ships very steady in bad weather. Siting the foremast immediately before the funnel looked strange when these vessels first appeared, but anticipated a popular post-1945 rig. A cowl on the funnel, a short mainmast and curved stem gave *Champlain* quite a different appearance from *Lafayette*. Appointments were the finest of any Cabin Class liner proper. On 17 June 1940 *Champlain* was sunk by a magnetic mine off La Pallice while carrying evacuated personnel from St.

Nazaire. She foundered in 20 minutes and about 300 refugees and 30 crew lost their lives.

[145] *NORMANDIE* 1935–41 St. Nazaire
79,300t. 981 × 118 3–2* TE–4 29½k.

Normandie which represented the French reply to *Queen Mary* [23] was laid down five months after the British ship, although completed a year earlier. Construction proceeded very slowly at one stage but never actually stopped. The French Government gave financial help from the beginning and state aid was so extensive that Gallic wit dubbed *Normandie* 'la dette flottante'. Size of *Normandie* and *Queen Mary* was the minimum considered consistent with the speed required and the Transatlantique and Cunard estimates of that size were alike. *Queen Mary* started with the larger gross tonnage, but enclosure of additional space raised the French liner to 83,400. The Cunarder's length between perpendiculars was 975 feet (6 less than *Normandie*) by pre-1955 rules, but beam six inches more; length overall measured 1017½ feet compared with the French 1027. Any suggestion that one ship was faster than the other ignores the vagaries and uncertainties associated with record-passages. The rivals could not have been more evenly matched. There, however, the similarity between the two liners ended.

Queen Mary was evolutionary, a natural development on her predecessors; the French liner, revolutionary. Streamlining in *Normandie* was carried to the limit and much of her auxiliary machinery and fittings was novel. The outstanding feature of the St. Nazaire masterpiece lay in the turbo-electric propulsion system which had hitherto been limited to 22,500-ton liners of much less speed. A marked difference from *Queen Mary* was the space allocation to the different passenger Classes and greater dependence on the First.

The keel-plate of *Normandie* was laid on 26 Jan. 1931 and the launch took place 29 Oct. 1932. She averaged 31 knots over several hours on trials and at 29 burned no more oil than *Ile De France* at 23½. A clipper stem with a pronounced curve terminated underwater in a bulbous forefoot and *Normandie* had a pronounced sheer forward. Bows were turtle-backed for a short distance and the sides of the hull nowhere parallel. The stern was elliptical, whereas *Queen Mary*'s of the cruiser type. Funnels were rather stumpy, pear-shaped and markedly stepped, and the third was a dummy. Fire-proof bulkheads and decks ensured that any fire could be localised.

Normandie replaced the *France* of 1912 and sailed independently of *Paris* and *Ile De France*. Leaving Havre on her maiden voyage, 29 May 1935, she immediately broke the Norddeutscher Lloyd *Bremen*'s records with ease and also demonstrated an advantage of her turbo-electric drive. The 'teething troubles' inevitable in any new ship necessitated cutting out a turbo-alternator for a short while, but the liner continued running on all four screws. On her first six round-voyages *Normandie* averaged 28·3 knots and throughout 1937 (18 voyages) 28·87. Modifications aft and changed propellers reduced vibration although this always gave some trouble. Behaviour in bad weather proved excellent and the sheer forward cut pitching to a minimum. Record passages appear under *Queen Mary* on page 34.

Fast though *Normandie* showed herself to be, the outstanding feature was the luxury of her accommodation which has never been equalled. She carried 848 First, no Second, 670 Tourist and 454 Third. Under a decision of the North Atlantic Passenger Conference (*see Queen Mary*) the First Class accommodation was renamed Cabin, but the generous lay-out, furnishings, etc. obviously remained superior to *Queen Mary*'s best which had been designed as Cabin Class from the start. Moreover, *Normandie* allocated 43 per cent of her 1970 berths to the most expensive category and the British liner only 36 per cent of her 2140. *Normandie* catered specially for the more moneyed traveller; *Queen Mary* had the wider appeal.

A consort planned after loss of *Paris* would have been larger than *Normandie*. Her name was to have been *Bretagne*, overall length 1148 feet and beam 138. Construction had to be deferred because the only building-slip at St. Nazaire for a hull of these dimensions was occupied by an aircraft-carrier.

When the 1939–45 War broke out *Normandie* was laid up at New York and she stayed alongside her pier after *Queen Mary*'s departure for Sydney. The United States seized *Normandie*, 12 Dec. 1941, and set to work converting her to the troopship *Lafayette*. Alterations entailed changes on the upper boat-deck and, in anticipation of completion, mattresses for 12,000 troops had been stacked on the promenade deck below. On 9 Feb. 1942 sparks from a blow-lamp fell among the mattresses and the entire deck was soon burning. The fire would probably have burned itself out, but knowledge of *Normandie*'s construction was lacking and tons of water were poured into the ship. The day was bitterly cold and water froze in the scuppers as it escaped from the vicinity of the blaze. Hoses from fire-floats and the shore continued to discharge water into the upper works until the excess top-weight caused *Normandie* to roll over and sink at her berth. Raising the hull in September 1943 was a triumph of marine salvage but the outlay of further labour, materials and money could not be justified. The wreck was therefore left until sold for breaking up three years later.

[146] *DE GRASSE* ('24) 1938–40, 1947 Birkenhead
Can. Pac. *EMPRESS*
OF AUSTRALIA 1953–55
17,750t. 552 × 71 2–2 GT–2 16k.

The French Government requires that Transatlantique ships should normally be built at home, but immediate post-war conditions caused the order for this Cabin Class ship to be placed in Britain. Name first intended was *Suffren*. *De Grasse* ran on the Havre–New York route until relief by *Champlain* in 1932. Employment then became cruising and seasonal trans-Mediterranean work.

De Grasse was restored to the New York service to replace the lost *Lafayette*. The Germans found *De Grasse* at Bordeaux, used her for accommodating submarine crews and scuttled the ship when they evacuated the port. The French refloated and reconditioned her with substantial alterations. Tonnage became 19,400 gross and the ship a one-funneller.

First Cie. Gle. Transatlantique post-war passenger sailing for New York was taken by *De Grasse* on 12 July 1947, berthing 711 passengers in two Classes

(First and a superior Tourist). She was transferred to the West Indies service at end of the 1951 season. The Canadian Pacific bought her in March 1953 as a temporary measure to bridge the gap between burning of *Empress of Canada* [47] and completion of *Empress of Britain* [52]. She was re-registered under the name *Empress of Australia* and worked in the Liverpool–Canada trade until December 1956. A second sale made her *Venezuela* of the Grimaldi Siosa Lines and she went to shipbreakers after running ashore near Cannes in March 1962.

LIBERTÉ 1950–61 *See EUROPA* [186]

[147] *FLANDRE* 1952–62 Dunkirk

20,450t. 568 × 79 1–2 GT–2 22k.

Flandre and a sistership, *Antilles*, were ordered for the West Indies service, but *Flandre* re-allocated to the New York as she approached completion. Main machinery and electrical installation incorporated many novel features and she broke down on her maiden Atlantic crossing, July 1952. *Flandre* finally reached New York in tow of a tug and on return home was sent back to the builders for repairs and alterations. Second departure for the United States took place at the end of April next year and she gave no further trouble. In conjunction with *Ile De France* and *Liberté* she permitted weekly Havre–New York sailings. *Flandre* possessed 212 First Class and 511 Tourist berths, but many of the latter began by being interchangeable. During the winter months she usually augmented *Antilles*' West Indies sailings and *Flandre* was transferred outright to the Caribbean service at close of the 1962 season. The summer of 1967 she made two special Havre–Montreal voyages. Early in 1968 the Cie. Gle. Transatlantique sold her to the Italian-owned Costa Line ('Linea C') and present name is *Carla C.*

[148] *FRANCE* 1962– St. Nazaire

66,350t. 952 × 111 1–1 GT–4 31k.

Largest liner in the world since sale of the Cunard *Queen Elizabeth* and also the fastest designed strictly for commercial purposes. *United States* [102] is indeed faster, but was built with potential employment as a troopship as a primary factor. *France* cost about £29 million of which the French Government paid £7–8 million. The first plate was laid on 7 Sept. 1957, the ship launched on 11 May 1960 and maiden departure for New York took place 3 Feb. 1962, after a short cruise to the Canaries.

France broke away from the Cie Gle. Transatlantique policy of cultivating First Class custom rather than the less expensive and the change of direction extended to abolishing Second altogether. Of her 2000 passengers 1500 are Tourist Class. Accommodation for the 500 First equals any on the Atlantic, but key-note of the decorations has become modernity instead of the 'elegance' in the company's earlier ships. *France*'s eight boilers generate the same power as *Normandie*'s 29 though oil consumption is reduced by 40 per cent. The 'wings' on the funnels are a conspicuous feature. They are in fact tunnels, designed to spread the emission of smoke clear of the ship. *France* was planned to make 23 transatlantic round-voyages a year which would provide an annual total of berths exceeding *Ile De France* and *Liberté* combined. Trial speed averaged 34 knots. She was publicised when new as 'the longest liner in the world' which was rather misleading since it referred only to overall length (1035 feet) and it was not until *Queen Elizabeth*'s withdrawal in 1968 that *France* became the world's largest passenger ship.

During her first 12 months *France* steamed 158,000 miles and averaged 30·3 knots, but no outstandingly fast passage has been attempted. Occupation of 80 per cent of passenger capacity over the full year, including the slack winter period, demonstrated this liner's popularity. *France* now does some winter cruising and made three special voyages to Quebec in connection with the 1967 Montreal Exhibition. She has been singularly free of the mechanical trouble often associated with new ships.

HOLLAND-AMERICA LINE (1874) *Dutch*

FUNNEL – *Yellow with green-white-green bands*

FLAG – *Horizontal stripes of green, white and green; black letters 'NASM' on the white*

HULL – *Black with an orange riband until 1951 when changed to plain grey (except* Noordam *and* Westerdam)

The Dutch were the first nation to realise that the Hudson River was the gateway into North America and in 1629 established at its mouth the settlement which was destined to grow into New York, New Amsterdam. Against such a background it would indeed have been strange if they had failed to create one of the main steamship companies linking Europe with New York. The way of the Holland-America Line, owned by the Netherlands-American Steam Navigation Company (Nederlandsch-Amerikaansche Stoomvaart Maatschappij) of Rotterdam, has, however, been far from easy. Lack of government financial aid such as has helped launch and sustain other Western Ocean Lines has been a relatively minor factor. The real difficulty has lain in Rotterdam's inadequate access to the sea which persisted over many years. The Dutch company began with two small emigrant-carriers in 1872 when improvements were being made to the New Waterway which joined the port to the North Sea and their significance may be gauged from the fact that the Holland-America named their third ship, *W. A. Scholten*, after the engineer who carried out the work. Even then further improvements were necessary before the New

Waterway could take larger vessels and from 1892 to 1893 these had to work from Amsterdam instead of Rotterdam. A ding-dong struggle with the rival port of Antwerp (represented by the Red Star Line) followed. Calls at French and British ports started at an early date, although the ports varied.

The 1920's found the Holland-America in a happier position than in earlier years. The Red Star was then in rapid decline. In 1902, 51 per cent of the capital had been acquired by the American-owned International Mercantile Marine Company, but the Dutch had repurchased this in 1917. An important consequence of reversion to full Dutch ownership was freedom to build ships in Holland instead of being tied to the Harland & Wolff yard at Belfast. The Rotterdam–New York passenger service was weekly with Boulogne and Plymouth calls, and Southampton replaced Plymouth westbound in 1923. Two large liners with extremely comfortable accommodation alternated their sailings with those of a smaller pair. At the end of the 1930's two motor vessels were placed on the direct Rotterdam–New York route, continuing to Philadelphia. The Holland–America bought the remains of the Red Star Line in June 1939, integrated the two steamers into their fleet and kept them running on the Antwerp–New York route under the old name.

Holland-America liners gave invaluable service as World War II troopships, etc., but the German assault on Rotterdam, May 1940, brought destruction of the big *Statendam* which had been the pride of the fleet over most of the 1930's.

Maiden post-war New York passenger sailing was mid-1946. Intermediate calls in the English Channel were changed to Havre and Southampton both ways. During the 1950's many Western Ocean passenger companies fitted second-hand liners with accommodation in which the ratio of First Class to Tourist was very small, but the Holland-America's *Ryndam*, *Maasdam* and *Statendam* were unique in being new ships berthing many hundred Tourist Class and under 100 First. The *Statendam*, lost in 1940, was replaced by the magnificent *Rotterdam*, a funnelless ship, in 1959.

Irish calls, either Cobh or Galway, started in 1952 and their frequency increased. A one-ship Canadian service started in April 1960 with sailings to Quebec and Montreal for eight months a year and to Halifax and New York for four, but the winter voyages ceased after three years. From 1963 these Canadian voyages began and ended at Bremerhaven with Rotterdam a port of call additional to Havre and Southampton. Acquisition of the Europe-Canada Line (*see* page 136) showed further interest in the German emigrant traffic.

Holland-America liners cruise extensively, but three sailed regularly to New York during the 1968 season and *Maasdam* to Montreal. A much-reduced pattern of transatlantic voyages was adopted for the 1969. *Rotterdam* was withdrawn for cruising, *Nieuw Amsterdam* took regular New York sailings and *Statendam* of 1957 a few. Intermediate calls became Southampton and Cobh with frequent additions of Havre and Halifax. The St. Lawrence passenger trade was dropped completely.

In 1967 the Holland-America Line took the very popular step of abolishing tipping in its ships. The building of a replacement for *Nieuw Amsterdam* is under consideration.

North Atlantic passenger liners form only a fraction of the fleet. Holland-America cargo ships are distinguished by names suffixed '– – – – – *dyk*' and operate a variety of services to North and Central America. Among them are many 'Twelves'. The company is also a member of the Atlantic Container Lines consortium.

[151] *ROTTERDAM* 1908–39 Belfast

24,150t. 650 × 77 2–2 4E–2 17k.

Until 1929 *Rotterdam* was easily the largest ship the Holland–America had ever owned. Accommodation was 555 First with 1120 Tourist and Third Class and she remained coal-fired to the last. Outbreak of World War II extended her life by a few months, but *Rotterdam* was scrapped in January 1940.

[152] *VOLENDAM* 1922–51 }
[153] *VEENDAM* 1923–53 } Clyde (H. & W.)

15,450t. 550 × 67 2–2* GT–2 15k.

Despite small dimensions this pair carried three passenger Classes and in the early 1930's berthed 263 First, 428 Second and 484 Tourist. *Veendam* picked up many survivors from the British aircraft-carrier *Courageous*, torpedoed off Land's End, 17 Sept. 1939. The Germans later seized *Veendam* at Rotterdam and used her for accommodating submarine crews. *Volendam* was fortunately at sea when the Germans invaded Holland and afterwards used to evacuate British children across the Atlantic. She had 271 adult passengers and 335 children on board and was in convoy bound for Canada when hit by a torpedo 200 miles north-west of Bloody Foreland, 30 Aug. 1940. All passengers were successfully transferred to other ships and the damaged liner beached on Bute. *Volendam* was commissioned as a troopship, July 1941.

After hostilities the Dutch Government chartered *Volendam* for carrying settlers to Australia and she did not resume running to New York for her owners until 1947. Refitting was only partial and she carried 1682 passengers in a single 'austerity' Class. *Veendam* returned to the Rotterdam–New York trade in January the same year, fully reconditioned for 223 First and 363 Tourist.

[154] *STATENDAM* 1929–40 Belfast and Schiedam
29,500t. *670* × 81 3–2* GT–2 19k.

One of the most handsome ships on the Atlantic and *Statendam* also had the reputation of being the most economical liner of her size. She was ordered at Belfast to replace a rather larger but slower namesake which had been commandeered by the British Government and sunk as the troopship *Justicia*, July 1918. The new *Statendam* was launched in September 1924, but work then ceased until she was towed to Holland for completion April 1927. Original accommodation was modified in the early 1930's to become 453 First Class, 793 Tourist and 418 Third. A decision to lay her up in September 1939 proved unfortunate. *Statendam* found herself right in the centre of the Rotterdam fighting, 10 May 1940, was set on fire, blazed for five days and was burnt right out.

[155]	*MAASDAM* ('21)	1934–41	7900t. 450 × 58 1–2 GT–1 13k.
[156]	*LEERDAM* ('21)	1934–54	
[157]	*EDAM* ('21)	1934–54	
[158]	*SPAARNDAM* ('22)	1934–39	

Originally 2-funnelled 8850-ton ships in the Mexican trade. Reconstructed, 1934, with 30 Cabin and 60 Third Class berths. Subsequent voyages were usually to New York or Baltimore. *SPAARNDAM* was sunk by magnetic mine in the Nore, 27 Nov. 1939, and *Maasdam* by submarine in the North Atlantic on 26 June 1941.

[159] *NIEUW AMSTERDAM* 1938– Rotterdam
36,300t. 670 × 88 2–2 GT–2 20½k.

Of the many North Atlantic liners used for World War II troop-carrying only *Nieuw Amsterdam* remains in service. The name first contemplated was *Prinsendam*, but that of the original New York is certainly happier and more appropriate. A proposed sister-ship was never built owing to the outbreak of war. For the first months of the 1939–45 War *Nieuw Amsterdam* alternated between pleasure-cruising in the Caribbean and a berth in the Hudson. Later she was converted to a troopship at Halifax and had a similar history to the Cunard '*Queens*'.

Nieuw Amsterdam was reconditioned at Rotterdam for 553 First, 443 Second and 207 Tourist Class travellers and resumed New York sailings on 29 Oct. 1947. The Second Class was eliminated at the end of 1961 and passenger capacity became 574 First and 583 Tourist with many berths interchangeable so that she could carry 260 First and 973 Tourist as an alternative. A defective boiler necessitated cancellation of three voyages, August–September 1967. After some hesitation the Holland–America Line decided to reboiler *Nieuw Amsterdam* and bring her thoroughly up-to-date.

[160]	*NOORDAM*	1938–63	Rotterdam
[161]	*ZAANDAM*	1939–42	Schiedam

10,800t. 475 × 64 1–2 M–2 17k.

Although primarily cargo ships the two *Noordam*s berthed 160 passengers in what was really a superior Tourist Class. Their route was Rotterdam–New York–Philadelphia but employment elsewhere after the 1940 spring. *Zaandam* was torpedoed in the South Atlantic on passage from Capetown to New York, 2 Nov. 1942. She sank within 10 minutes and 124 of her 169 passengers and 130 crew were lost.

Noordam returned to ordinary commercial employment in January 1946. She sailed between Rotterdam and New York, but called at Havre for a time. Sold to become the Panamanian *Oceanien*.

WESTERNLAND, 1939–40; *PENNLAND*, 1939–41.

See Nos. 206 and 207

[162]	*WESTERDAM*	1946–64	Schiedam
[163]	(*ZUIDERDAM*)		Schiedam

12,150t. 491 × 66 1–2 M–2 16k.

Broadly similar to *Noordam*, though with less speed. *Westerdam* (134 First) and a sister, *Zuiderdam*, were launched after the Germans had occupied Holland. The Dutch resistance movement defeated every attempt to complete the ships. *Westerdam* was scuttled three times, but finally salved after the liberation and her arrival at New York on 8 July 1946 was the first post-war of a Holland–America passenger vessel. The Germans sank *Zuiderdam* to block the New Waterway and, although raised in 1946, she was found beyond repair.

[164]	*RYNDAM*	1951–66, 1968–	Schiedam
	Eur. Can. *RYNDAM*	1966–67	
[165]	*MAASDAM*	1952	
	Pol. Ocean		
	STEFAN BATORY	1969–	

15,000t. 476 × 69 1–2 GT–1 16½k.

854 Tourist Class with 39 First at approximately Second Class fare. *Ryndam* was ordered as *Dinteldyk*, a 11,200-ton cargo steamer, but altered to a totally different ship soon after construction commenced. From 1960 she ran in the Canadian service and *Maasdam* replaced her in 1967. *Maasdam*'s voyages usually began at Bremerhaven from 1963. On 13 Feb. 1963 *Maasdam* struck the wreck of the British *Harborough* off the Weser Lightship and damaged herself so severely that she had to be towed into Bremerhaven for repair. *Ryndam* and *Maasdam* both made winter New Zealand voyages in the later 1960's.

Ryndam was transferred to the Europe–Canada Line and German registry in the 1966 autumn. She undertook educational cruises from the United States until April 1967 and regular Bremerhaven–New York voyages followed. In September 1967 *Ryndam* became the Transocean Steamship Company's *Waterman* (*see* page 120), but reverted to the Holland–America flag and her old name after 12 months. Present employment consists of more American educational cruises.

Maasdam went to the Polish Ocean Lines at end of the 1968 season, though service as *Stefan Batory* did not commence until 1969.

[166] *STATENDAM* 1957– Schiedam

24,300t. 578 × 79 1–1 GT–2 19k.

Statendam (84 First, 867 Tourist) was built in dry-dock. Maiden sailing from Rotterdam took place in February 1957 and she cruised from New York until May. *Statendam* represents the *Ryndam* idea of a mainly Tourist Class ship transferred to a vessel with the size and speed more generally associated with present-day passenger liners.

[167] *ROTTERDAM* 1959– Rotterdam

38,650t. 650 × 94 0–1 GT–2 20½k.

The premier Holland–America liner. In *Rotterdam* twin-exhausts abreast take the place of a funnel, an arrangement which has improved internal lay-out. The Netherlands Government helped finance construction to the extent of roughly one-third, partly as compensation for destruction of *Statendam* [154] and partly as a loan. Much of *Rotterdam*'s accommodation is interchangeable and she can carry either 580 First Class with 789 Tourist or 301 with 1060. Mean speed on trials exceeded 23½ knots.

Rotterdam started her maiden voyage, 3 Sept. 1959 and has made several winter world cruises. Her 1969 schedule includes one transatlantic round-voyage, but otherwise consists of Caribbean cruises from New York.

PRINSES MARGRIET 1963, 1965–67 *See* No. 178

NETHERLANDS GOVERNMENT AND TRANSOCEAN STEAMSHIP COMPANY (1951–1963) *Dutch*

FUNNEL – *Yellow with narrow red-white-blue bands and black lip.*

FLAG – *Orange with a narrow red-white-blue horizontal stripe one-third from the top.*

HULL – *White with green waterline.*

Holland was compelled to encourage large-scale emigration to help solve post-war economic problems and to this end the Netherlands Government established its own line of emigrant vessels.

Operation was in 1961 transferred from the Directorate General of Shipping to a mainly government-owned company, the Transocean Steamship Company (Scheepvaart Maatschappij Trans-Oceaan).

The Government passenger fleet comprised three converted ex-'Victory' ships and most voyages were across the North Atlantic from Rotterdam, but many were to South Africa or Australia. Management and manning of the individual vessels were entrusted to various private companies with the Holland-America acting as general agents for the North American sailings. In early years 20 or more Western Ocean voyages were made annually and shared equally between Montreal with a Quebec call and New York with an outward stop at Halifax. Sailings gradually dropped to eight a year and 1960 saw the last two to the St. Lawrence. The ships occasionally touched at Havre and Southampton. Sailings ended in 1963 and the westward Halifax call had been abandoned some time before. Each vessel began by berthing about 900 passengers, most of them in 'dormitories'. Fares were the lowest on the Atlantic and corresponded with the Greek Line's smaller ships. Although the service was created for the benefit of Dutch emigrants, berths were freely bookable and some voyages made specially for students. The Netherlands Government augmented the fleet by chartering two old liners for a period. One made a fair number of Atlantic voyages, but the 12,350-ton motorship *Sibajak* only three (in 1954–55). In 1961 improvements to the former 'Victory' ships increased the proportion of passengers berthed in cabins and reduced the total number to around 820.

See under *Groote Beer* for the 'Atlantic Educational Program Foundation' of 1964–66.

Ryndam [164] was transferred from the Europe–Canada Line to a temporarily revived Transocean Steamship Company in September 1967, renamed *Waterman* and painted Transocean colours. She made some New York voyages for students, but berths were not available to the general public and the arrangement lasted only a year.

[171]	*ZUIDERKRUIS* ('44)	1951–61	Portland, Oregon
[172]	*GROOTE BEER* ('44)	1952–63	Richmond, Cal.
[173]	*WATERMAN* ('45)	1952–63	Portland, Oregon.

9150t. 437 × 62 1–2 GT–1 16k.

Originally called *Cranston Victory*, *Costa Rica Victory* and *La Grande Victory*.

The Dutch names were those of the star-constellations Southern Cross, Great Bear and Aquarius respectively. Only 1951 North Atlantic sailing was made by *Zuiderkruis* to Quebec in July.

Over half the St. Lawrence and New York voyages were taken by *Groote Beer* under Holland–America Line management, although this ship made one or two winter voyages to Capetown. *Zuiderkruis* and *Waterman* divided their employment between the North Atlantic and the southern routes. *Zuiderkruis* made no American voyages after 1961 and was transferred to the Dutch Navy for use as a depotship, January 1963. A Greek shipowner, John S. Latsis, bought her sisters at end of that year and *Waterman* was renamed *Margareta*.

Groote Beer kept her Dutch name under Greek ownership and her funnel was painted plain yellow. She was chartered for three or four Rotterdam–New York voyages a year in 1964–66 for the 'Atlantic Educational Program Foundation', catering for students. Passages were offered to the general public and the Holland–America Line again acted as agents.

[174] *JOHAN VAN OLDENBARNEVELT* ('30) (0) 1955–58 { 19,800t. 588 × 75
2–2 M–2 15½k.

On long-term charter from the Nederland Line and managed by that company. *Johan Van Oldenbarnevelt* made about two New York voyages annually for four years at lower speed than the ex-'Victory' ships. She remained painted Nederland colours.

The Holland–America had chartered this liner directly after outbreak of World War II for two or three Rotterdam–New York voyages. The Greek Line bought the ship in 1963 and converted her for cruising from Southampton under the name *Lakonia*. Destroyed by fire at sea at end of the year.

ORANJE LINE (1953–1963) *Dutch*

FUNNEL – *Yellow with lozenge and monogram of the house-flag*

FLAG – *Orange with blue lozenge and white monogram*

HULL – *Grey with green waterline*

The Oranje Line (originally owned by Anthony Veder & Company, later by the Maatschappij Zeetransport) is a cargo concern trading to Eastern Canada. For a time it possessed three small motorships with passenger licences and it remains unique in having carried passengers from Europe through the St. Lawrence Seaway to Great Lakes ports. The original route was from Rotterdam to Montreal or to Halifax and St. John, according to season, but later vessels continued from Montreal to Toronto and

Chicago. The Oranje ships generally called at Plymouth (Southampton westbound in later years) and added Havre to their itinerary in 1960.

[176] *PRINS WILLEM VAN ORANJE* 1953–61 { 7350t. 431 × 62 1–2 M–1 16½k.

60 First Class. *Prins Willem Van Oranje* proceeded no further than Montreal until 1959, but afterwards occasionally went through to the Great Lakes. Was reduced to a 'Twelve' at end of 1961 and became East German *Ferdinand Freiligrath* three years later.

[177] *PRINSES IRENE* 1959–63
[178] *PRINSES MARGRIET* 1961–63
Hol. Am. *PRINSES MARGRIET* – 1963, 1965–67
} Hardinxveld
8550t. 420 × 61 1–2 M–1 16½k.

Prinses Irene (115 First) and her sister were specially designed for the Great Lakes trade, although the first voyage (April 1959) was to Montreal only. *Prinses Margriet* was chartered to the Holland–America for four Rotterdam–New York passenger voyages in 1963 and both ships made their last Oranje sailings that year.

The Holland–America Line chartered the pair in 1965, but used them for cargo only. The Holland–America then bought *Prinses Margriet* and put her back on the Rotterdam–New York route as a passenger ship. The Indonesian Djakarta Lloyd purchased *Prinses Irene* and renamed her *Tjut Njak Dhien. Prinses Margriet* remains the property of the Holland-America, although chartered by the Royal Netherlands Steamship Company in 1968 for a New York–West Indies service.

CHAPTER V

German Lines

NORDDEUTSCHER LLOYD – HAMBURG – AMERICAN LINE – BERNSTEIN LINE – BERNSTEIN (RED STAR) LINE – GERMAN ATLANTIC (formerly HAMBURG ATLANTIC) LINE – EUROPE–CANADA LINE

NORDDEUTSCHER LLOYD (1858–1914, 1922–1939, 1954–)
German-West German

FUNNEL – *Deep yellow-ochre*

FLAG – *White; blue anchor-and-key design*

The German mercantile marine is characterised by the dominance of two companies, the Norddeutscher Lloyd of Bremen and the Hamburg-American. Bremen and Hamburg resemble each other in being city-states which include a detached strip of territory at the river mouth and have utilised this to establish an outport. The cities proper must always be understood as including their respective outports of Bremerhaven and Cuxhaven, although actual relationship differs. The largest Hamburg ships can proceed up the Elbe to Hamburg and normally begin and end their voyages there, though they tend to handle passenger traffic at Cuxhaven. Really large vessels, however, cannot reach Bremen and so for passenger liners Bremen has always meant Bremerhaven, 35 miles further down the Weser.

Bremerhaven is closer to the open sea than Hamburg and hence developed into the German leading passenger port. Hamburg's compensating advantage consists of magnificent network of wide and deep waterways (natural and artificial), ideally suited for barge traffic deep into Czechoslovakia or eastwards into what is now Poland. With two brief breaks Bremerhaven has been the home of the speediest German transatlantic liners and Hamburg the port of a heavier type of ship in which cargo received greater attention.

The Norddeutscher Lloyd's earlier years contained two peak periods. In the latter 1880's, the heyday of single-screw, ex-Bremerhaven steamers gave Southampton two departures a week by fast liners. Other companies possessed larger and faster vessels, but none had a bi-weekly service of the Norddeutscher Lloyd calibre. Bremerhaven's temporary inability to handle twin-screw ships led to a passing Hamburg-American superiority, but 1898 gave the Bremen line the first non-British Atlantic record-breaker since the days of the paddlers, *Kaiser Wilhelm Der Grosse.* This ship and two improved editions were the North Atlantic's swiftest liners until commissioning of the *Lusitania* pair.

Bremerhaven's position as Germany's premier passenger port has never been more obvious than during the past four decades. Hamburg had nothing to compare with the Norddeutscher Lloyd's 'Blue Riband' holders, *Bremen* and *Europa* of 1929–30, nor even with the relatively slow *Columbus.* Throughout the 1930's the three Lloyd liners maintained weekly Bremerhaven–Southampton–Cherbourg–New York sailings, though *Columbus* only fitted into the schedule with great difficulty. Unfortunately, the record-breakers could hardly have entered service at a less fortunate moment, for the World Depression had begun. Receipts fell and the Norddeutscher Lloyd was heavily involved in a bank failure. Yet worse was to follow the Nazi accession to power. All those free-born men and women who refused to blind themselves to the obvious shunned the abhored Swastika emblem wherever it flew and *Columbus* actually berthed at Bremerhaven on one occasion with only seven First Class passengers on board. Non-German lines gradually recovered from the terrible early 1930's though neither the Norddeutscher Lloyd nor the Hamburg–American did so. Virtual nationalisation was required to save Germany's two giant shipping companies from bankruptcy, but national prestige demanded the building of a liner to offset the British, French and Italian 'greyhounds' which had deprived *Bremen* and *Europa* of their laurels. When World War II began the Norddeutscher Lloyd had planned a 80,000-ton ship capable of a maximum sea-speed exceeding 36 knots. *Viktoria*, as she was to have been called, would have been driven by five screws and measured 1000 feet between perpendiculars with 111 feet beam, but construction was never started.

Nearly five years of war were to end with loss of the Lloyd's entire fleet and this allows a retrospect of the organisational changes which had interlocked the Bremen line and the Hamburg-American during the preceeding years although their separate identities had been outwardly retained. The two companies combined have long accounted for the larger portion of German mercantile tonnage and their activities, often competitive, have been world-wide with Western Ocean passenger tonnage forming only part of their fleets. *Europa*'s completion in 1930 gave the Lloyd 149 ships totalling over 860,000 tons and the Hamburg Fleet at this date was rather larger. That year worsening trading conditions forced the rivals to come together in a loose organisation termed a 'Union' which meant little more than co-ordinating services, etc. Outstanding liabilities, mainly in the United States, continued to pile up until government intervention became essential. In 1932 each company was compelled to reduce its capital by two-thirds in return for financial aid and guarantees from the Reich and a consortium of banks. Revenues of other transatlantic shipping concerns began to show signs of recovery in 1933, but world revulsion against the Hitler regime caused Germany's Western Ocean passenger revenues to fall by one-third from the low 1932 level. The financial position became desperate and direct Reich intervention inevitable, the process being called the 'Sanierung' (literally, 'restoration to health'). The Bremen and Hamburg giants were restricted to the long-distance trades and their lesser vessels passed over to other companies. The Lloyd fleet declined to 68 ships totalling 562,000 tons. More spectacular and significant was a financial reconstruction. The 1932 capital adjustment had already deprived the unfortunate shareholders in each instance of two shares out of three and the 1934 required them to surrender four out of every five shares of the reduced capital. The Nazi Government assumed direct responsibility for the two companies' debts and received shares in compensation. For the Norddeutscher Lloyd the final result of this remarkable operation was that the capital became 45 million marks of which 33 million belonged to the state. Figures for the Hamburg-American Line were almost identical. The Government had thus become overwhelmingly the majority shareholder in each company with power to make appointments to the boards accordingly. The private shareholders' representatives could be ignored and services continued regardless of the mounting financial losses.

The Bremen and Hamburg companies still remained separate, but there was also an unpublicised internal arrangement whereby, for financial purposes and no other, each transatlantic passenger fleet was 'hived off' and the two were united as the 'North Atlantic Partnership'. This device cleared the way for ultimate separation from the parent-companies. In 1941 Hitler's Reich sought ready cash for armament production and to this end declared the 'Sanierung' complete. By a procedure called 'reprivatisierung' (English, 're-privatisation') the state sold its Norddeutscher Lloyd and Hamburg-American holdings to private interests. At the same time the 'North Atlantic Partnership' was converted into a third and separate company, the German America Line, half owned by the state and half equally divided between the Lloyd and the Hamburg-American. To the German-American Line Bremen contributed *Europa* and *Berlin* (*Bremen* and *Columbus* had already been lost) and Hamburg the four *Albert Ballin* liners and *St. Louis*. None of these ships were ever again to cross the Atlantic under a German flag—*Europa* had to be handed over to the victors and the others became casualties in the war's closing stages—and so the German-America Line came to naught.

Recovery of German shipping after the 1945 overthrow was slow. The Norddeutscher Lloyd was bereft of all its surviving ships for a second time and reconstruction of the cargo fleet, obviously the first consideration, did not commence until 1951. Re-entry into the Atlantic passenger trade took place early in 1954 with acquisition of *Gripsholm* (renamed *Berlin* the next year) from the Swedish Amerlcan Line. She had become too old and slow for the Swedes who parted with her under special arrangement whereby they retained half-ownership for five years. Routeing was direct from Bremerhaven to New York until later years when *Berlin* touched at Southampton outward and homeward during the height of the season. A new *Bremen* hoisted the Norddeutscher Lloyd house-flag in 1959. She, too, was second-hand, but had been completed on the very eve of World War II. Seven years afterwards a second acquisition from the Swedish American, *Kungsholm* of 1953 (renamed *Europa*), permitted retirement of the aged *Berlin*. *Bremen* and *Europa* work along the same Bremerhaven–Southampton-Cherbourg–New York track of their famous pre-war namesakes. Winter employment is cruising.

[181] *GENERAL VON STEUBEN* ('23) 1931 Stettin
STEUBEN 1938–45
14,700t. 526 × 65 2–2* 3E–2 16k.

Reconstruction of the Norddeutscher Lloyd passenger fleet after World War I commenced with the 13,350-ton sisters, *München* and *Stuttgart.* Their design was severely utilitarian and *Stuttgart* relegated to the Far East service at the end of the 1932 season.

München was brought home and largely rebuilt after being burned at New York in 1930. Furnaces were converted to burn oil and the funnels replaced by two of greater height and girth. Passenger accommodation was changed to 420 Cabin Class and the name to *General Von Steuben* after the Prussian soldier who trained Washington's armies. She then became the company's regular cruising-liner, but made occasional New York voyages. The year 1938 saw her name shortened to plain *Steuben* in deference to Nazi suggestions that an officer who had left the Prussian army to serve a foreign country was unworthy to be given his military rank. A Russian submarine torpedoed and sank *Steuben* off Stolpmünde shortly before dawn on 20 Feb. 1945. She had embarked 4000 refugees from East Prussia and only about a quarter of them survived the disaster.

[182] *COLUMBUS* 1923–39 Danzig
32,550t. 750 × 83 2–2 GT–2 22k.

In 1912 the Norddeutscher Lloyd planned two cheaper versions of the White Star *Olympic*, reducing both size and speed. The first was launched in December 1913 and eventually surrendered to become the British *Homeric* [17]. Her sister was laid down the following year, but so little progress had been made with construction in 1919 that the Germans succeeded in retaining possession. Although the name *Hindenburg* had been provisionally allocated, she received that of the surrendered ship, *Columbus.* Originally intended to burn coal, she was changed to oil-firing while building. *Columbus* left Bremerhaven in December 1923 on her maiden voyage, propelled by triple-expansion machinery. Maximum sea-speed amounted to about 19 knots. An outstanding merit was stability in all weathers and she remained Germany's finest liner until 1929.

Towards the end of 1927 *Columbus* wrecked one of her two 16,000 I.H.P. main engines and this was temporarily replaced with one of 6000 belonging to another ship. She then ran at reduced speed for over a year. In 1929 *Columbus* was temporarily withdrawn from service for an extensive refit to bring her more into line with the record-breakers, *Bremen* and *Europa.* The reciprocating machinery was replaced by single-reduction geared turbines and boiler power increased. Broader and much shortened funnels brought a resemblance to *Bremen.* She rejoined the mail service, December 1929, with 22 knots speed and berths for 480 First, 610 Tourist and 596 Third Class. *Columbus* first took refuge at Vera Cruz when World War II broke out. From there she attempted to run back to Germany, but the British destroyer *Hyperion* intercepted her 300 miles off the Virginian coast on 19 Dec. 1939 and she scuttled herself to avoid capture. The American cruiser *Tuscaloosa*, which was shadowing, rescued the crew.

[183] *BERLIN* 1925–45 Bremen (Vulkan)

15,300. 549 × 69 2–2* 3E–2 16½k.

An oil-fired and improved edition of *München*. *Berlin*, operated as an 'intermediate' in the 1930's with accommodation for 257 Cabin Class, 261 Tourist and 361 Third, was chartered for workers' cruising early in 1939. She lay in a fjord near Kirkenes as a hospital ship for much of World War II and in the final stages was used for the evacuation of German refugees from the eastern Baltic. On 1 Feb. 1945 *Berlin* struck two mines near Swinemünde and foundered.

The Russians salved *Berlin* in 1948–49 and reconstructed her in such leisurely fashion that she was not again ready for sea until 1957. She is now the Russian passenger ship *Admiral Nakhimov* and stationed in the Black Sea.

[184] *DRESDEN* ('15) 1927–34 Bremen (Vulkan)

14,150t. 550 × 67 2–2 4E–2 15k.

A coal-burner and originally the Norddeutscher Lloyd's own *Zeppelin*, this ship had been surrendered in 1919 without taking a sailing. She was bought back from the Orient Line who called her *Ormuz*. By 1934 *Dresden* was used entirely for pleasure-cruising. She sank in Bokn Fjord, Norway, on 21 June 1934 after hitting a rock the previous day.

[185] *BREMEN* 1929–41 Bremen (Weser)

[186] *EUROPA* 1930–45 Hamburg (Blohm & Voss)

C.G.T. *LIBERTÉ* 1950–61

51,650/49,750t. 899/890 × 102 2–2 GT–4 27½k.

The *Lusitania*/*Mauretania* pair reigned unchallenged as the Atlantic's fastest 'greyhounds' from 1907 until advent of the German *Bremen* in mid-1929, but 22 years of Cunard speed supremacy were largely due to a fortuitous circumstance. An Atlantic liner's speed must allow her to leave Europe at a convenient hour and yet to be taken up-harbour soon after arrival off New York. Any extra speed which brought her off that port in darkness would merely result in having to anchor until daylight. Consequently a point is reached where relatively small speed-increases bring no advantage and a really big 'jump' becomes essential. *Bremen*'s 27½ knots represented the minimum worthwhile increase on *Mauretania*'s 24/25 and passage of time was needed before such an increase became practicable. Even then the German constructors had to accept a 'longer ship' (i.e. a greater ratio of beams to length) than either the *Mauretania* or the *Normandie* and *Queen Mary* of the 1930's.

A debenture issue floated in the United States provided the necessary money and *Bremen* and *Europa* were laid down in July 1927. Construction which involved many innovations proceeded rapidly and both were launched 14 months later. *Bremen* commenced her maiden voyage, 16 July 1929; *Europa* was seriously damaged by fire while fitting-out and did not take her initial sailing until 20 March 1930. The two liners were not identical. Tonnages and lengths differed and are shown above. An obvious difference appeared in the funnels which in *Bremen* were pear-shaped, whilst *Europa*'s were oval and 10 feet higher.

Stream-lining was marked and funnels of both ships were so low that they had to be heightened 15 feet within a few years. Each vessel berthed approximately 600 First, 500 Second, 300 Tourist and 600 Third Class. *Bremen* won the Atlantic speed-record either way on her first voyage—4d. 17h. 42m. (27·83 knots) from Cherbourg to the Ambrose and 4d. 14h. 30m. (27·91) from Ambrose to the Eddystone. Next year *Europa* improved a little on the westward time and speed. The fastest crossing of all was *Bremen*'s eastward in June 1933—4d. 12h. 15m. (28·51 knots).

A cruise round South America took *Bremen* through the Panama Canal, February 1939, and made her the largest commercial ship to have used that waterway. On 1 Sept. that year she slipped out of New York without passengers and reached Murmansk safely. *Bremen* returned to Bremerhaven down the Norwegian coast, 10–13 Dec., and was lucky to escape attack by the submarine *Salmon* on the passage. She joined *Europa* at Bremerhaven where some desultory attempts were made to fit out both as troop transports and eventually abandoned. On 18 March 1941 a mentally unbalanced seaman set *Bremen* on fire in course of a personal feud with another crew-member. The burning liner had to be scuttled and was afterwards found beyond repair. *Bremen* was therefore stripped down to the waterline and the hull finally demolished in 1953. *Europa* was moved from the Weser to Hamburg to obtain greater immunity from air attack. When hostilities ended *Europa* and *Milwaukee* [198] were the only German North Atlantic passenger liners remaining afloat. Examination of *Europa* led to a startling discovery. The long hull was structurally weak and had been stiffened with additional plating. The remains of *Bremen* revealed similar strengthening. The Americans took *Europa* over for repatriating their troops, but after two voyages they had no further interest in the ship because of the expense involved in essential reconstruction.

In May 1946 *Europa* was awarded to France, moved to Havre and renamed *Liberté* for the Cie. Gle. Transatlantique two months later. The night of 9 Dec. 1946 she broke adrift in a gale and collided with the wreck of *Paris*. A hole torn in *Liberté*'s starboard side necessitated scuttling to prevent capsizing. The ship was subsequently raised and taken to St. Nazaire for such drastic reconstruction that she emerged with speed reduced to 23½ knots on a tonnage of 51,850 gross. *Liberté* (569 First, 562 Second, 382 Tourist Class) entered the Havre–New York trade with a sailing on 17 Aug. 1950. Heightening the funnels during the annual 1953–54 refit finally destroyed any resemblance to the streamlined record-breaker *Europa*. After leaving Havre, 27 Dec. 1956, *Liberté* sustained such serious weather-damage that she was forced to return to port. *Liberté*'s final voyage ended at Havre on 16 Nov. 1961.

	GRIPSHOLM	1954	*See GRIPSHOLM* [322]
	BERLIN	1955–66	
[187]	*BREMEN* ('39)	1959–	St. Nazaire

32,350t. 670 × 88 1–2 GT–4 23k.

The massive *Bremen*, the Norddeutscher Lloyd's fifth ship of that name, is the largest and finest German liner today. She started her career as *Pasteur* of the Cie. de Navigation Sud-Atlantique and outbreak of war caused cancellation of maiden sailing for Buenos Aires. Employment from August 1940 to June 1945 was as a British troopship under Cunard management. On release the French used *Pasteur* for trooping to Indo-China, but she was laid up at Brest early in 1957 and offered for sale.

The Norddeutscher Lloyd bought the unwanted ship, September 1957, and re-registered her as *Bremen.* She was moved to Bremerhaven where new engines and boilers were installed and the entire interior reconstructed to accommodate 216 First and 906 Tourist Class passengers, though external appearance showed little change. For a vessel of this size the high ratio of Tourist berths to First is very noticeable and the quadruple screws are unusual. *Bremen* initiated her service under the German flag with a departure for New York on 9 July 1959.

EUROPA 1966– *See KUNGSHOLM* [327]

HAMBURG AMERICAN LINE (1856–1914, 1922–1939)
German

FUNNEL – *Buff with black-white-red bands at the top*

FLAG – *Quartered diagonally, white (top and bottom) and blue; shield, yellow; anchor and letters, black*

The Hamburg-American Line (Hamburg-Amerikanische Packetfahrt Aktien-Gesellschaft, briefly called the 'Hapag') occupies an unusual position among present-day Atlantic shipping companies in having begun in sail. It was founded in 1847, but the canvas era lasted only a short time. Emergence as a real rival to the Norddeutscher Lloyd for the high-grade transatlantic passenger traffic is attributable to Albert Ballin whose brilliance and achievements were such that his name has eclipsed the founders'. Not only did Ballin make his shipping company the world's largest, but in 1914 the Hamburg-American had become Germany's premier Atlantic passenger carrier.

The 'Hapag' recovered a prominent position among the North Atlantic lines between the World Wars, but made no attempt to win the passenger willing to pay the highest rates. Four vessels of the mid-1920's remained the backbone of the transatlantic passenger fleet until German shipping was swept off the seas for a second time. Their route was Hamburg–Southampton–Cherbourg–New York and they were much improved in the early 1930's. Passengers were usually embarked and landed at Cuxhaven, 65 miles lower down the Elbe than Hamburg where voyages began and ended. Two Cabin Class motorships added in 1929 provided a secondary New York service.

Organisational history of the Hamburg-American after formation of the Third Reich resembled the Norddeutscher Lloyd's.

World War II and its immediate aftermath wiped out the entire 'Hapag' fleet and subsequent rumours of projected North Atlantic passenger liners proved groundless. The German Atlantic Line whose ships it provides with officers must be considered the 'Hapag' successor in the Western Ocean passenger trade. The Hamburg-American Company has, however, fully recovered its old prominence among the leading owners of freighter tonnage and operates two New York joint-services in conjunction with the Norddeutscher Lloyd—one with 'Twelves' and the other with container-ships.

[191]	*ALBERT BALLIN*	1923	Hamburg (Blohm & Voss)
	HANSA	1935–45	
[192]	*DEUTSCHLAND*	1924–45	

21,000t. 646 × 73 2–4* GT–2 19½k.

See HAMBURG (below).

The first vessel's name was changed to *Hansa* on account of Albert Ballin (died, 1918) being of Jewish origin. *Deutschland* had a serious fire at sea in October 1938.

[193]	*HAMBURG*	1926–45	Hamburg (Blohm & Voss)
[194]	*NEW YORK*	1927–45	

22,100/22,350t. 646 × 73 2–2* GT–2 19½k.

For all practical purposes *Albert Ballin*, *Deutschland*, *Hamburg* and *New York* formed a single class, although small differences existed. They were ugly and drastically utilitarian ships with relatively greater cargo capacity than their Bremen contemporaries. They underwent two major reconstructions. Original length was 602 feet and speed only 15½ knots. *Albert Ballin* and *Deutschland* measured 20,700 gross tons; the second pair averaged 21,300. A unique feature was a blister fitted with hydrostatic valves and designed to minimise rolling. It increased overall beam to 79 feet and extended along half the length amidships. Ships' sides were slightly corrugated about the waterline, funnels stumpy and bolt-upright, and sterns of the cruiser-type. The obvious external differences between the pairs lay in the number of masts and shape of the funnels. The *Albert Ballin*s had oval funnels; the *Hamburg*s, squarish with flat sides. Original accommodation (First, Second and Third) also differed, the first two carrying many more Third Class than *Hamburg* and *New York*.

At 15½ knots the quartette were too slow and installation of more powerful machinery and new boilers in 1929–30 raised speed by 4 knots. Putting the discarded engines into 'Hapag' cargo steamers under construction reduced the cost of the changes. Hull alterations followed four years afterwards. A new bow added 44 feet to length and increased tonnages to the figures shown. Hull-form was so greatly improved that speed remained unchanged though oil expenditure fell 20 per cent. Height of the funnels had been increased in 1929–30 and this with the extra length bettered appearance considerably. Accommodation settled down to roughly 200 Cabin Class, 360 Tourist and 400 Third.

In September 1939 the westbound *New York* made for Murmansk. From there she slipped back to Hamburg at end of the year and was later moved to Altenfjord to house workmen engaged in repairing the damaged battleship *Tirpitz*. The quartette were sent to the Baltic in 1945 to carry troops and stores to the Russian Front and return with evacuated persons, but the Royal Air Force quickly ended their activities. *Hansa* was sunk by mine near Warnemünde on 6 March 1945 and *Hamburg* off Sassnitz the next day. Air attacks accounted for *New York* at Kiel on 3 April and *Deutschland* near Lübeck, 3 May.

The Russians raised and reconstructed *Hansa* and *Hamburg* though the work proceeded very slowly. The former *Hansa* emerged in 1955 as *Sovetsky Sojus*, again a passenger ship though with masts reduced to two and funnels to one. Reconstruction of *Hamburg* as the factory ship *Yuri Dolgurky* took even longer.

[195] *RESOLUTE* ('20) 1926–35 Bremen (Weser)
[196] *RELIANCE* ('20) 1926–38 Geestemünde
19,700t/19,550t. 596/592 × 72 3–2* 3ET–3 17k.

These ships were laid down for the Hamburg–American Line before World War I under the names of *William O'swald* and *Johann Heinrich Burchard* and belonged to a trio intended to inaugurate a luxury service to Buenos Aires. The third vessel became the British *Empress of Australia* [44] and differed from this pair in having extra beam and unorthodox machinery. Construction was suspended shortly after war started but the two smaller ships were transferred to the Dutch on the stocks as compensation for tonnage sunk by submarine after being guaranteed a safe conduct. They were completed as *Brabantia* and *Limburgia* for the Royal Holland Lloyd's Plate trade, although modified to reduce topweight. One deck was eliminated and height of the funnels reduced, whereas *Empress of Australia* was finished to the original design. The standard of accommodation remained exceptionally high, although not quite on a par with the liner surrendered to Great Britain. Funnels were very widely spaced. Two were fed by uptakes split at main deck level and the third served as a ventilator.

The Allied Powers refused to recognise transfer of these liners which incidentally had proved too ambitious for the South American trade. They were therefore sold in 1922 to the United American Lines, a corporation formed to operate between New York and Hamburg in association with the 'Hapag'. The American owners called the ships *Resolute* and *Reliance* respectively, converted them to burn oil and remodelled the accommodation to berth 290 First Class travellers, 320 Second and 400 Third. The United American Lines closed down after the 'Hapag' had re-established itself and sold both vessels to the Hamburg–American, July 1926.

Resolute and her sister continued on the Hamburg–New York route and later made possible the temporary withdrawal of the four *Albert Ballin*s during their re-engining and lengthening refits. They were frequently used pleasure-cruising and *Reliance*, painted white, exclusively after 1935. At the time of the Abyssinian War, Italy was seeking to buy old liners for use as troopships and purchased *Resolute*. The Italians called this ship *Lombardia* and lost her, 4 August 1943, during an American air raid on Naples. Fire gutted *Reliance* at Hamburg, 10 August 1938 and she was sold for breaking up.

[197]	*ST. LOUIS*	1929–44	Bremen (Vulkan)
[198]	*MILWAUKEE*	1929–45	Hamburg (Blohm & Voss)

16,700t. 545 × 72 2–2* M–2 16k.

The motorships *St. Louis* and *Milwaukee* (270 Cabin Class, 287 Tourist, 416 Third) were almost as ugly as the steam-driven *Albert Ballins*. They derived their names from American cities with an unusually strong German element in their population. They were built for a supplementary New York service and frequently made calls at Cobh and Halifax. Increasing world understanding of the Nazi regime made *Milwaukee* redundant and she became a regular cruising ship with her hull painted white.

St. Louis was among the German liners which were at sea when the 1939–45 War started and found their way home via Murmansk. The German Navy made her into an accommodation ship at Kiel where she was almost destroyed by aerial bombing on 30 August 1944. The remains were taken to Hamburg and the after-part utilised as a hotel until scrapped six years later. *Milwaukee* survived the war, did some American trooping and was finally allocated to Great Britain. She was renamed *Empire Waveney* and destroyed by fire at Liverpool, 1 March 1946, while undergoing conversion to a regular troopship.

[199]	*VATERLAND*	Launched 1940	Hamburg (Blohm & Voss)

c. 36,000t. *c.* 740 × 98 2–2 TE–2 23k.

Ordered May 1939 as the first of three sisters to replace the *Albert Ballin* class vessels. In September 1940 she was launched without ceremony to clear the slip. This ship was referred to as 'No. 523' and never named, although there seems no doubt that *Vaterland* was intended. She received a hit during an air raid on 27 July 1943, burned for several days and ended a total loss.

BERNSTEIN LINE (1931–1939) *German*

FUNNEL – *Black with house-flag narrowly edged with white*

FLAG – *Black and red, white diamond, black letters*

The Bernstein Line (Arnold Bernstein Reederei) of Hamburg was unostentatious, but possesses points of interest. It began in 1926 and was the only successful transatlantic shipping company built up between World Wars I and II without any form of subsidy or other government encouragement. Success largely turned on active co-operation between a shipping and a North American railway company—an arrangement which had once been common, but died out in the early 1900's. The Bernstein Line commenced as a purely cargo concern, operating between Antwerp (occasionally Hamburg) and New York. The ships were small second-hand steamers, specially adapted for the carriage of unpacked automobiles. An association was formed with the Erie Railroad early in 1930 whereby the railway company provided extra capital and the two co-operated in handling cargo passing between points on the Erie Railroad and Europe. A year later three Bernstein steamers were fitted with very limited passenger accommodation.

The Bernstein passenger-freighters sometimes called at Havre or Southampton. Fares were low and for some years the company remained outside the North Atlantic Passenger Conference. In 1935 Arnold Bernstein, the founder, enlarged his interest in the Western Ocean passenger trade through purchase of the long-established Red Star Line (*see* the next Sub-Chapter). He was a non-Aryan and imprisoned by the Nazis two years later. Collapse of the Bernstein Line followed and the ships were sold to breakers in June 1939.

[201]	*GEROLSTEIN* ('04)	1931–39	7750t.	454 × 56	1–2	4E–2	13k.
[202]	*ILSENSTEIN* ('04)	1931–39	8200t.	448 × 56	1–2	3E–2	13k.

Originally the Shaw Savill *Mamari* and *Matatua*, bought 1928–29, renamed and enlarged. Demolition of *Ilsenstein* was stopped and in 1940 she was sunk as a blockship in a Scapa Flow entrance.

[203]	*KÖNIGSTEIN* ('07)	1931–39	9650t.	459 × 60	1–2	3E–2	13½k.

Previously *Arawa* and acquired from the Shaw Savill Line at the same time as the preceding ships, although a better type of vessel. She had been a regular passenger liner in the New Zealand trade with over 300 berths distributed in three Classes. Demolition of *Königstein* was halted by the Belgian shipbreakers October 1939, and she was reconstructed to become the freighter *Gandia* of the Cie. Maritime Belge. Sunk by submarine, January 1942.

BERNSTEIN (RED STAR) LINE (1935–1939) *German*

FUNNEL – *Black with red star on white band*

FLAG – *On a white burgee, a red star*

The Bernstein (Red Star) Line was a direct continuation of the original Red Star Line which had operated passenger ships between Antwerp and New York under the same flag for over half a century. It began in 1873 as a Belgian company with Belgian promoters, though much of the money was American. Earliest voyages were to Philadelphia, but others to New York were added at an early date and Philadelphia eventually dropped altogether. By the 1890's the Red Star had become entirely American-owned, though the ships kept their Belgian registration. British-flag ships crept into the Red Star and from 1924 onwards the whole fleet stood on the British register with the exception of two aged emigrant-carriers. All subsequent replacements consisted of unwanted British ships from other member-companies of the International Mercantile Marine. The trade connection withered away until in 1934 only the former White Star liners, *Westernland* and *Pennland*, were still running. In February the following year they were sold to Arnold Bernstein together with the Red Star name and goodwill.

The new acquisition was kept separate from the original Bernstein Line and a new company, the Bernstein (Red Star) Line, created to take over the Red Star, though again much capital came from American sources. *Westernland* and her sister which had hitherto carried three passenger Classes were modified to take Tourist Class only. The Antwerp–Southampton–New York route with frequent westbound Halifax calls was kept and the ships sometimes visited Boston. *Westernland* left Antwerp for the first time under the new auspices, 30 March 1935.

In June 1939 the Holland-America bought the Red Star Line and absorbed the two ships into their own fleet. The Red Star organisation ceased to be, but the Antwerp–New York service continued under the old designation.

[206]	*WESTERNLAND* ('18)	1935	Clyde (H. & W.)
	Holl–Am. *WESTERNLAND*	1939–40	
[207]	*PENNLAND* ('22)	1935	Belfast
	Holl–Am. *PENNLAND*	1939–41	

16,300t. 575 × 68 2–2* 3ET–3 15½k.

538 Tourist Class. *Westernland* which began as the Dominion Line's *Regina* was transferred to the White Star in 1925 and the Red Star in 1930 when also renamed. *Pennland*, originally *Pittsburgh*, ran for the White Star until re-allocation to the Red Star in 1925 and her name was changed the year following. *Westernland* was oil-fired and her sister coal.

The Holland–America Line retained the Red Star funnel and hull-colour for some months after acquisition. The two steamers became troopships in 1940 and *Pennland* was sunk from the air in the Gulf of Athens, 25 April 1941. The British Admiralty purchased *Westernland*, November 1942, for conversion to a depotship, but the work was not carried out and she continued trooping. Broken up, 1947.

EUROPE-CANADA LINE (1955–1967) *West German*

FUNNEL – (a) *Blue with black lip*

(b) 1966. *Yellow with ring of large white diamonds on a green band*

FLAG – *Nine chequers—four green and four white; the central chequer, red with a green maple leaf enclosed in white diamond*

HULL – *White with black waterline, but* Ryndam *kept Holland-America colours*

The Europe-Canada Line belonged to the Europe-Canada Line Company of Bremen and first departure was Bremerhaven–Havre–Southampton–Quebec–Montreal by *Seven Seas* on 30 April 1955. For the early sailings the ship was on charter and flew the Panamanian flag. Transfer to German registration did not take place until immediately before her fourth departure for Canada and the funnel and flag shown above were not adopted until 1956. Prior to this the blue funnel had carried a script monogram 'ECL' in white and there had been no house-flag. The Holland-America and Rotterdam Lloyd jointly bought the business in October 1955 and eight years afterwards the Holland-America acquired full proprietorship. The Europe-Canada however remained a German-registered company with *Seven Seas* and her successor Bremen registered and manned. Calls at intermediate ports varied, though Rotterdam and/or Zeebrugge became pretty regular. Winter voyages were to Halifax and New York. Transfer of the Rotterdam Lloyd *Willem Ruys* to the Europe-Canada Line was contemplated in 1958, but the idea dropped after she had made two Bremerhaven–Montreal voyages.

The Canadian immigration boom passed and in 1961 *Seven Seas* began making summer voyages to New York. The St. Lawrence was abandoned altogether in 1963 and New York substituted. The ship became increasingly used for student cruises from American ports and transatlantic voyages fell to two a year. Replacement of *Seven Seas* by *Ryndam* in mid-1966 brought better accommodation and more sailings, and the Europe-Canada Line quietly altered its name to the E.C.L. Shipping Company. Sailings ceased at close of the 1967 summer season.

[211] *SEVEN SEAS* ('40) 1955–66 Chester, Pa.
11,750t. 465 × 70 1-1 M-1 15½k.

Originally the United States escort-carrier *Long Island*, converted in 1949 to the Panamanian *Nelly* for charter. *Seven Seas* carried 1066 Tourist Class, mainly in 'dormitories', and 25 passengers in a very cheap First. Accommodation was improved and the numbers slightly reduced within two or three years. *Seven Seas* was on passage to New York when on 17 July 1965 an engine-room fire deprived her of power 500 miles east of St. John's and a tug had to be sent to tow her to Newfoundland. Rotterdam University bought the ship the summer of 1966 for use as a students' hostel.

RYNDAM 1966–67 *See* No. 163

GERMAN ATLANTIC (formerly HAMBURG ATLANTIC) LINE

(1958–1968) *West German*

FUNNEL – *Red with white Hanseatic cross and narrow black top (see* Hanseatic *illustration on page 91)*

FLAG – *On red, a white Hanseatic cross*

HULL – *Light grey with narrow blue riband from* 1967.

The Hamburg-American Line made no attempt to restore its New York passenger service after World War II and Home Lines filled the gap in 1951 with *Italia* and the 'Hapag' acting as their German agents. By 1957 a larger vessel became desirable and Hamburg dissatisfied with dependence on a foreign company. Upshot was formation of the German-registered Hamburg Atlantic Line with capital provided by Home Lines, the city of Hamburg and private German subscribers. The Canadian Pacific's *Empress of Scotland* was bought, extensively refitted as *Hanseatic* and on 21 July 1958 inaugurated a new Cuxhaven-New York service by way of Havre and Southampton. She was mainly Tourist Class and the line's only ship, but proved popular and profitable. Winter employment was cruising. Cherbourg was substituted for the

Havre call in April 1962. The name of the line was changed to German Atlantic (Deutsche Atlantik Linie) at the end of 1965 by which time all connection with Home Lines had ceased.

Active life of the original *Hanseatic* ended with a disastrous fire, September 1966. The German Atlantic immediately contracted for a replacement (*Hamburg*) and arranged to charter cruising ships while she was building. Within a few months, however, the Zim *Shalom* was bought for delivery in late 1967. She, too, received the name *Hanseatic*. With her the company returned to the New York trade the spring of 1968 and *Hamburg* was due to commission 12 months later. Negotiations began with the Norddeutscher Lloyd for a fully integrated New York joint-service, made considerable progress and then broke down. Under these circumstances the German Atlantic decided to withdraw from the transatlantic business altogether. Final departure of the second *Hanseatic* from New York for Cuxhaven was on 6 September 1968.

The German Atlantic now uses its ships for pleasure-cruising from European and American ports. They are officered and manned by the 'Hapag'.

HANSEATIC 1958–66 *See EMPRESS OF SCOTLAND* [51]

HANSEATIC 1967– *See SHALOM* [304]

[216] (*HAMBURG* 1969–) Hamburg (Deutsche Werft)

23,500t. 638 × 87 1–1 GT–2 22k.

Finished as a regular cruising-liner, although ordered as a dual-purpose ship. *Hamburg* is a conventional ship, but a peculiar and ugly funnel sited a long way aft gives an unusual profile. She crossed to New York, June 1969, after a cruise in the Mediterranean.

CHAPTER VI

Lines with North-Western European Services Under 'Flags of Convenience'

GREEK LINE – HOME LINES – INCRES LINE – AROSA LINE

GREEK LINE (1939–) *Greek-Panamanian-Liberian*

FUNNEL – (a) *Yellow with black top and broad blue band; on the blue, a white* 'Γ'

(b) 1953. *As above, but* 'Γ' *replaced by the yellow device of the house-flag*

FLAG – (a) *On blue, a white* 'Γ'

(b) *Blue, yellow device with 'ropework' base of pale blue and yellow*

HULL – *White for Canadian ships,* Olympia *and all later vessels*

The Greek Line belongs to the General Steam Navigation Company of Greece, founded by the Goulandris Brothers, and the 'Γ' on the former funnel and house-flag represents the Greek 'G'. The line is based on Piraeus and began in 1937 with the departure from that port for New York of *Nea Hellas*, an ex-Anchor steamer. World War II caused suspension of sailings from 1941. Operations were resumed five years later and acquisition of further second-hand tonnage then commenced. The Greek Line originated the practice, since adopted by other companies, of buying unwanted passenger liners and refitting them mainly with Tourist Class accommodation for further employment, often under 'flags of convenience'.

A striking development took place in 1950 with the decision to take advantage of the German emigration boom and absence of German passenger shipping from the Atlantic. That year the Greek Line commenced sailings by Panamanian-registered ships from Bremerhaven to the St. Lawrence and Bremerhaven–New York voyages followed the next year. Main activity was shifted to the northern services and soon three ships were working from Bremerhaven under the Panamanian flag compared with the solitary *Nea Hellas* from Piraeus under the Greek. The Bremerhaven–New York route received *Olympia* late in 1953, straight from the builder and far superior to existing tonnage. With *Olympia* the Greek Line introduced a third national flag into their fleet by placing her on the Liberian register.

The Bremerhaven vessels had polygot crews. Officers were Greek; their stewards, cooks and pursers' staffs were German; other crew members were a mixture of Greeks and Italians. The St. Lawrence terminal, originally Montreal, was changed to Quebec and there were no winter sailings to Canada. Usual calls were Southampton, Cherbourg and Cobh. The New York liners had a similar itinerary in European waters, but added Halifax on their outward passages. From 1956 some voyages on either northern route were made via Southampton, Liverpool and Dublin. The year before *Olympia* and the veteran *Nea Hellas* (renamed *New York*) had exchanged stations in order to meet Home Lines' competition from Piraeus. In 1958 *Arkadia*, flying the Greek ensign, took over all the Canadian sailings and provided improved accommodation although the route was altered to Bremerhaven–London–Havre–Cobh–Quebec–Montreal before the year was out. This Canadian service was discontinued in 1966 and the Bremerhaven–New York had terminated seven years earlier.

Olympia, still on the Liberian register, and a second modern liner (*Queen Anna Maria*) now comprise the Greek Line fleet and charge similar passage rates to the majority of transatlantic shipping companies. Both have Greek crews. Piraeus remains the home port, although Haifa has been the eastern terminal on most voyages since 1961. The normal route is now Haifa–Limassol–Piraeus–Messina–Naples–Lisbon–Halifax (westbound)–New York, but is subject to some variation. Palermo is a frequent addition and some voyages include Boston homeward. *Olympia*'s main employment became cruising in 1968.

	NEA HELLAS	1939	*See TUSCANIA* [62]
	NEW YORK	1955–61	
[221]	*KATOOMBA* ('13)	1946–47	Belfast
	COLUMBIA	1949–59	

9400t. 450 × 60 1–2 3ET–3 13½k.

An Australian coastal steamer bought from the Australasian United S.N.

Company. *Katoomba* re-opened the Greek Line's Piraeus–New York service in 1946, but was chartered the next year by the Cie. Gle. Transatlantique for their West Indies trade. On conclusion of the charter she was refitted at Genoa, converted from coal to oil-burning and renamed *Columbia.*

Columbia (52 First, 750 Tourist) reverted to the Piraeus–New York route, but is believed to have made some 1949 voyages to Central America. Features common to this and the two following vessels were that registration was in the name of a subsidiary company domiciled in Panama, First Class fares were low and most of the Tourist Class passengers were berthed in 'dormitories'. *Columbia* opened the Greek Line's Bremerhaven–Canada service in June 1950 and continued running to Canada until November 1957 when laid up at Piraeus. Most of her 1957 sailings were from Liverpool with a Belfast call.

[222] *NEPTUNIA* ('20) 1949–57 Amsterdam
10,450t. 506 × 59 1–1 3E–2 14½k.

Neptunia (39 First, 725 Tourist) came from the Nederland Line who had known her as *Johan De Wit.* She started by running from Piraeus, but was re-allocated to the Bremerhaven–New York service in April 1951. *Neptunia* took the place of *Canberra* on the Canadian route after sale of the latter, although she acted as temporary relief for *New York* on the New York run each winter. She struck Daunts Rock outside Cobh, 2 Nov. 1957, while on passage to the United States and was beached in consequence. Although refloated, *Neptunia* was at once sold to shipbreakers.

[223] *CANBERRA* ('13) 1949–54 Stephen
7700t. 410 × 57 1–2 4E–2 13½k.

Another acquisition from the Australian coastal trade. Previous owners were the Australian Steamship Proprietary Company. The Greek Line retained the name, fitted 64 First and 648 Tourist Class berths, and adapted the furnaces to burn oil. *Canberra* was moved from the Piraeus–New York run to the Bremerhaven–Canada in the spring of 1951. At close of the 1954 season the Dominican Government bought her for carrying migrants from Spain under the name, *España.* She lasted until 1959.

[224] *OLYMPIA* 1953– Stephen
23,000t. 560 × 79 1–2 GT–2 21k.

Built to Greek Line order for the Bremerhaven–New York service and much superior to the second-hand ships. *Olympia* was launched without a name and her owners wished to call her after Frederica, Queen of the Hellenes, but registration in Liberia rendered this impracticable. She was the earliest North Atlantic liner designed from the outset to cater mainly for Tourist Class travellers (*see*, however, the Holland–America *Ryndam* [163]), though much accommodation is interchangeable. Passenger capacity is either 227 First and 1084 Tourist or 50 and 1261.

Olympia's maiden voyage, October 1953, began from Southampton. She was transferred to the Mediterranean route in March 1955 and had her hull painted black for the next two or three years. Principal employment since the beginning of 1968 has been cruising and working between New York and Bermuda.

[225] *SKAUBRYN* ('51) (0) 1957
9800t. 458 × 57 1–2 M–2 16k.

A Norwegian ship with 'dormitory' accommodation, chartered in June–September 1957 for three round-voyages to Quebec from Bremerhaven and another from Liverpool.

[226] *ARKADIA* ('31) 1958–66 Tyne (Vickers)
20,250t. 553 × 77 1–1 TE–4 19k.

Arkadia (52 First, 1320 Tourist) was the first Greek Line vessel other than *Nea Hellas* to be registered in Greece and a big improvement on the Panamanian ships she replaced. She had been built as the 3-funnelled Furness liner *Monarch of Bermuda*, a most luxurious vessel for the New York–Bermuda trade. Navigational difficulties at Hamilton explain the quadruple screws which gave extra manoeuvrability. *Monarch of Bermuda* was gutted by fire, May 1947, while being reconditioned on the Tyne after trooping. Hull and machinery, however, remained intact and were bought by the Ministry of Transport for whom the wreck was re-built as *New Australia*, a totally different type of vessel. In her new role she carried government-sponsored emigrants to Australia. Profile was changed beyond recognition by giving her one big funnel and an ugly dipod mast which served as an additional smoke-outlet.

The Greek Line bought *New Australia* for their Canadian service and made some improvements. Maiden departure from Bremerhaven took place in May 1958 as *Arkadia*. She made two or three Australian winter voyages, but usually cruised to Las Palmas from December to March. As the 1960's progressed the annual number of Atlantic crossings was reduced and her cruising period extended. *Arkadia* was unexpectedly laid up in the Fal in mid–1966 and sold at the end of the year.

QUEEN ANNA MARIA 1965– *See EMPRESS OF BRITAIN* [52]

HOME LINES (1949–1965) *Panamanian-Greek*

FUNNEL – *Pale buff with blue top and ball-and-crown device of the house-flag* (*see* Atlantic *illustration on page 90*)

FLAG – *On white, a gold mural* (*turretted*) *crown inside a large blue ball*

HULL – *White with green waterline*

Most ambitious of the Western Ocean passenger concerns launched since World War II is Home Lines which captured a share of the higher-grade traffic for a while, although now confined to pleasure-cruising from New York. The company is registered in Panama, but so far as management and manning are concerned, may be considered as Italian-based on Genoa. One vessel, however, was transferred to a subsidiary, had a Greek crew and flew the Greek flag. Home Lines, like the General S.N. Company of Greece, began in the Mediterranean and afterwards took advantage of the absence of German passenger shipping to operate refurbished second-hand liners on northern routes to the Hudson and the St. Lawrence, but worked from Hamburg instead of Bremerhaven. Both employed German stewards, cooks and clerical staffs in their northern ships.

The money behind Home Lines is mainly Greek with a little Italian and possibly some American. The founder, Eugen Eugenides, was of Greek nationality and much of the original capital came from Sweden. Home Lines started as two separate companies—South Atlantic Lines and Panamanian Lines—which were worked as one and amalgamated in 1951. The Swedish-American Line provided two ships and owned 55 per cent of the South Atlantic shares, but withdrew on amalgamation. The Swedish influence can be plainly seen in Home Lines' name and funnel. The former is derived from the '-*Holm*' suffix of the Swedish fleet. The funnel at first had no blue top and was directly copied from the Swedish-American Line with the three crowns replaced by a single one of different design.

Home Lines were established to trade between Italy and Latin America under the Panamanian ensign and activities began with the despatch of *Argentina*, an ex-Norwegian vessel, from Genoa to Brazil and the River Plate in January 1947. The former Swedish-American ships followed next year. A fourth and much better liner was bought and should have joined them, but South American currency restrictions were causing difficulties and so Home Lines decided to try a new trade with the departure from Genoa for New York of *Atlantic*, 14 May 1949. The ex-Swedish pair joined her in 1950 and all three liners had their accommodation much improved during the 1950–51 winter. The following season they had to meet competition from fast new ships of the American Export Lines and Home Lines tried some experimental Hamburg–New York voyages. Next year brought total reorganisation of Home services with the entire fleet running to North America.

The Genoa–Naples–New York trade was left to the two oldest

vessels. *Atlantic* and *Italia* moved to northern waters and exchanged their Italian catering staffs for German, but were allocated different routes. The latter sailed between Hamburg and New York via Southampton, Havre and Halifax; *Atlantic*, between Southampton, Havre and Quebec. Transatlantic sailings ceased over the winter months and were replaced by pleasure-cruising. Home Lines attracted passengers prepared to pay higher rates than in the Greek Line ships. Both companies used second-hand vessels, but the Home were of much better stamp and so well re-equipped that they could charge fares corresponding with those of the major lines.

Atlantic had to contend with the Canadian Pacific and Cunard sailing schedules, each of which provided weekly departures for the St. Lawrence. She began and ended each season at Hamburg, but by making Southampton her usual terminal, 'turning round' at Quebec and carrying hardly any cargo, succeeded in reducing the interval between round-voyages to 16 days. *Homeric* relieved her after three years, was the fastest liner in the Canadian trade and from August 1957 proceeded up-river to Montreal. *Italia* was transferred to the same route except that voyages continued to start and finish at Hamburg.

Fresh employment for the displaced *Atlantic* had been found back in the Mediterranean. Still a Home ship, she was transferred to a Greek subsidiary company, given a Greek crew and renamed *Vasilissa Freideriki*. The ex-*Atlantic* then opened a Piraeus–Messina–Naples–Palermo–Gibraltar–Halifax–New York service and the Genoa–Naples–New York was dropped. Intermediate ports varied and sometimes included Boston. By 1960 all the shipping companies engaged in the Europe–Canada passenger trade were feeling the effect of a diminished demand for berths and Home Lines withdrew *Italia*, but extended *Homeric*'s route from Southampton across the North Sea to Cuxhaven. Quest for profitable employment for *Italia* brought a 10-year contract for regular winter sailings from New York to the Bahamas and these were made her responsibility.

Withdrawal from the St. Lawrence route, however, was the last thing contemplated at this stage, for Home Lines planned an attempt to capture transatlantic passenger traffic directly analogous with that made by the Canadian Pacific with *Empress of Britain* [49]. An outstanding vessel, *Oceanic*, was ordered, although destined never to be employed in the manner originally contemplated. Air-travel was making ever heavier inroads into the shipping companies' Canadian passenger receipts and the post-war rush of migrants across the North Atlantic had come to an end. Home Lines' Canadian bookings were halved between 1957 and 1962, and *Homeric* finished her last Montreal voyage in October 1963. The following year she relieved *Italia* on the far side of the Atlantic. *Vasilissa Freideriki* kept the Piraeus–New York service in being for two years longer, but was then sold to other operators, although she remained on the route. Her disposal at the end of 1965 concluded Home participation in the transatlantic passenger business. *Oceanic* was completed as a regular cruising liner, crossed to New York and there joined *Homeric.* Employment of the two liners remains the weekly New York–Nassau service and pleasure cruising in the West Indies.

[231] *ATLANTIC* ('27) 1949 Philadelphia
VASILISSA FREIDERIKI 1955
Chan. *VASILISSA FREIDERIKI* 1966–67
20,550t. 554 × 83 2–2 GT–2 20k.

(Generally referred to as *Queen Frederica,* although the registered name is *Vasilissa Freideriki.* The Greek name is painted on one side of the bow and the English variant on the other.)

Bought from the Matson Line and refitted at Genoa for the North Atlantic. Built as *Malolo* for the San Francisco–Honolulu trade, she had been the pride of the Matson fleet in her early years and in 1937 was re-registered as *Matsonia.* Two years back on her old route had followed wartime troop-carrying.

Atlantic (174 First and 1023 Tourist Class) started her Home career in the Genoa–New York service, but was switched to the Southampton–Quebec in 1952. She remained there for three years and was then transferred to a subsidiary company (the National Hellenic American Line) for operation between Piraeus and New York. As *Vasilissa Freideriki* this vessel was still a Home Lines' ship for all practical purposes, although Greek registered and manned.

Chandris Lines bought *Vasilissa Freideriki* and used her in the same manner as Home Lines for two seasons. Her present employment is in the Australian trade.

ITALIA 1949–60 *See KUNGSHOLM* [323]
BRASIL 1950 *See DROTTNINGHOLM* [321]
HOMELAND 1951–55
ARGENTINA 1952 *See BERGENSFJORD* [311]

[232] *HOMERIC* ('32) 1955– Quincy, Mass.
24,900t. 605 × 79 2–2 GT–2 21½k.

Homeric was originally the Matson *Mariposa,* one of three sisters which captured the entire passenger traffic between San Francisco and Australia. She became a World War II troopship and was afterwards laid up until bought by Home Lines for conversion to an all-passenger ship. Re-boilering and re-engining at San Francisco restored her speed and the accommodation was entirely rebuilt at Trieste. When finished, *Homeric*'s quarters for 147 First Class were second to none in the Canadian trade. Another 308 berths were interchangeable between the First and Tourist Classes, and beyond these *Homeric* carried 782 Tourist passengers. She relieved *Atlantic* on the Southampton–Quebec route and cleared the English port for the first time, 2 May 1955. Initial Home sailing had, however, taken place on 24 Jan. when she left Venice for pleasure-cruising from New York.

In her second year *Homeric* steamed from Rimouski to Havre in 4d. 23h. 25m., averaging a fraction over 22 knots and a post-war record which none of her British rivals have equalled. Final North Atlantic season began inauspiciously. Returning from a West Indies cruise, April 1963, *Homeric* damaged her rudder so badly that a new one had to be made at Quebec with the result that her first westward crossing was deferred six weeks. By this time her terminals had become Cuxhaven and Montreal. Since 1964 she has operated from New York, either running to Nassau or cruising further afield.

[233] *OCEANIC* 1965– Monfalcone

39,350t. 674 × 96 1–1 GT–2 26½k.

Oceanic is one of the largest and fastest liners afloat. A broad funnel set right aft gives her an unmistakable silhouette. She was ordered as a dual-purpose vessel, to cross from Europe to Quebec in comparable time with the 'greyhounds' running to New York and to cruise over the period the St. Lawrence is closed to navigation. Home Lines' decision to abandon the Canadian trade brought some minor changes in the design and *Oceanic* was completed as a regular cruising-liner. She sailed from Genoa for New York in April 1965 and has since worked from that port, winning a reputation as the most luxurious of the cruise-ships. Accommodation is for 1200 passengers in a single Class when cruising, but *Oceanic* carries 230 First and 1370 Tourist on her rare Atlantic crossings.

INCRES LINE (1950–1951) *Panamanian*

FUNNEL – *Buff with rather narrow blue top*

FLAG – *Quartered, white and red over blue and white*; *a black letter in each quarter* ('*I*', '*C*', '*D*' *and* '*N*')

The Incres Line began as a transatlantic passenger company, but has since turned to pleasure-cruising. It belongs to the Incres Compañia de Navegacion of Panama and the house-flag is the Panamanian national ensign modified to bear the company's initial letters. Founder was Arnold Bernstein of the Bernstein and Bernstein (Red Star) Lines and the Incres represented the first of two attempts to revive these. Bernstein had become an American citizen and the new company was really American. The founder's interest in the venture ceased after a few months. The route across the Atlantic was New York–Plymouth–Antwerp. The service which began in July 1950 was maintained by one ship, *Europa*, and lasted only 16 months. On one eastward crossing *Europa* had carried a single passenger. In 1951 three Antwerp–Plymouth–Montreal voyages were also made on Incres' behalf. These were carried out by the 30-year-old *Protea* on charter (*see Arosa Kulm* [236]).

[235] *EUROPA* ('23) 1950–51 Tyne (Vickers)
15,050t. 552 × 72 1–2 GT–2 15k.

Europa was the former P. & O. mail liner *Mongolia* and in 1938 had been transferred to the New Zealand Shipping Company as *Rimutaka*. The Incres Line equipped her as a one-Class ship, berthing 500 passengers at roughly Second Class fare. She was renamed *Nassau* in 1952 and used between New York and the Bahamas. The Incres company later sold the ship to become the Mexican *Acapulco*. Scrapped, 1964.

AROSA LINE (1952–1958) *Panamanian*

FUNNEL – *Buff with black ring close to top, black lip*

FLAG – (a) *Red and green separated by white diagonal stripe (similar to that of* 1954) *bearing the black letters 'CIT'*
(b) 1954. *Blue with white stripe and letters*

HULL – Arosa Kulm *had white hull with green riband and waterline for first two years. Otherwise hulls were black* (Arosa Sky, *grey*) *with or without white riband*

If ever a shipping line could fairly be described as multi-national, it most certainly was the Arosa. Headquarters were located on the shore of Lake Geneva and the name, Arosa, derived from the Swiss mountain overlooking the owner's home. The owner, Nicolo Rizzi, is understood to have been a Yugoslav national of Italian race. The Arosa ships were registered as belonging to the Compañia Internacional Transportadora of Panama and flew the appropriate ensign. Bremerhaven was their base and they were worked by mixed German and Italian crews. Two had originally sailed under American colours and two under French; one bore a German name and the others English. *Arosa Kulm*, the first steamer, had also flown the flags of Belgium and Honduras before passing to the Arosa Line. Perhaps it is not irrelevant to conclude that Switzerland created a small mercantile marine after the 1939–45 War, but has a stringent mercantile code which was hardly suitable for the Arosa fleet.

Purpose of the Arosa Line was to cater for the Canadian immigration boom of the early 1950's and the principal accommodation of the 'dormitory'-type *Arosa Kulm* was fifth-hand, another ship third-hand and the others second. The maiden sailing was Bremerhaven-Zeebrugge–Southampton–Halifax on 18 March 1952. Halifax continued to be the winter port, but the next voyage was made to Montreal. Quebec became the Arosa's St. Lawrence terminal after a year. Intermediate ports of call varied. Plymouth and London were successively tried, but Havre and Southampton eventually adopted as the usual calls. Some voyages were made via the Hook of Holland or Zeebrugge and others direct from Bremerhaven to Quebec or even by way of Gothenburg. The first two seasons were so profitable that they prompted expansion. Two more ships were bought and better accommodation provided, but enlarging the fleet coincided with contraction of the emigration surge from Germany. The Arosa had to compete with the Bremerhaven-based vessels of the more firmly established Greek Line, whilst the reviving Norddeutscher Lloyd deprived them of cargo. From mid-1956 Arosa passengers were again carried right through to Montreal and some voyages made to New York instead of the St. Lawrence. That winter's sailings were to St. John and Canadian winter voyages afterwards ceased altogether.

Waning St. Lawrence bookings caused a 1957 addition to the fleet to be assigned to the Bremerhaven–Havre–Southampton–New York route. By then the original steamer had been removed from transatlantic trading. The company's finances became more and more straitened and were not improved by letting the catering arrangements to an Italian firm. The 1957 acquisition had to be sold the following autumn and that December the other Arosa vessels were arrested for debt. On 10 April 1959 a Swiss judge declared the line bankrupt and the ships were sold to help meet liabilities of around £700,000. By a strange quirk of fate, however, *Arosa Sun*, freshly painted in Arosa colours and with name unchanged, can still be seen although no longer sea-going. She closes the story of this multi-national line by introducing yet another country—Holland.

[236] *AROSA KULM* ('20) 1952–56 Hog Island, Pa.
8950t. 436 × 58 1–2 GT–1 14½k.

Arosa Kulm (German, 'Summit of Mt. Arosa') began as *Cantigny* and *American Banker* [85] under the Stars-and-Stripes, but had three intermediate owners before purchase by the Arosa Line. She had been the Belgian *Ville D'Anvers*, the Honduran *City of Athens* and the Panamanian *Protea* in turn, and the Incres Line had chartered her as *Protea* the summer of 1951.

The Arosa company radically altered *Arosa Kulm* before her maiden sailing on their behalf. Fitting her with 46 Tourist Class berths in cabins and 919 in 'dormitories' entailed an enlarged superstructure. A broader though rather shorter funnel with slanting top replaced the earlier one and she finished with conventional pole-masts where the first and third 'goal posts' had been. Later *Arosa Kulm* received a few very cheap First Class berths and the 'dormitory' accommodation was reduced. Employment in 1957 and 1958 was voyaging to Australia or cruising out of Bremerhaven. *Arosa Kulm* was arrested for debt at Plymouth while on passage home from Jamaica and broken up in Belgium.

[237] *AROSA STAR* ('32) 1954–58 Quincy, Mass.
9050t. 423 × 60 1–1 GT–1 15k.

Bought from American owners who operated her between New York and Puerto Rico. Earlier names were *Borinquen* and *Puerto Rico*. Extensive reconstruction at Bremerhaven changed appearance completely. The single mast was stepped right forward, but a tripod structure rising from the bridge and carrying the radar apparatus could be mistaken for a second. *Arosa Star* had a passenger capacity of 38 inexpensive First and 768 Tourist Class. She cruised from New York in the latter part of 1958 and was arrested at Bermuda.

Buyers renamed this ship *Bahama Star* and kept her on the Panamanian register. She ran between Miami and Nassau until late in 1968.

[238] *AROSA SUN* ('30) 1955–58 St. Nazaire
16,250t. 575 × 68 1–2 M–2 16k.

Arosa Sun (60 First, 890 Tourist) had a better standard of accommodation than the earlier ships and was much larger. She came from the Messageries Maritimes who called her *Félix Roussel*. After World War II her French owners had replaced two hideous low square funnels with a single one of conventional shape. *Arosa Sun*'s first Atlantic crossing was actually to New York from Trieste where she had been refitted, July 1955. She lay at Bremerhaven when seized for debt 6 Dec. 1958.

A Dutch firm bought *Arosa Sun* to house their workmen and moored her in the North Sea Canal, a short distance above Ijmuiden. She remains in this position and outwardly looks very much the same as when she sailed for the Arosa Line.

[239] *AROSA SKY* ('49) 1957–58 La Ciotat
17,300t. 562 × 76 1–2 M–3 20k.

Also purchased from the Messageries Maritimes, though much superior to *Arosa Sun*. Construction had lasted ten years and been frequently suspended. The name under which launched in 1944, *Maréchal Pétain*, was changed to *La Marseillaise* before completion. France's loss of Indo-China rendered her unprofitable in the Far East trade.

Arosa Sky charged higher fares than earlier Arosa liners. Profile differed little from *Arosa Sun*. She sailed exclusively to New York and did some cruising from that port. Maiden voyage from Bremerhaven commenced 10 May 1957. *Arosa Sky* was sold, October 1958, to become the Italian *Bianca C*. On 24 Oct. 1961 she caught fire at sea and foundered off Grenada.

Chapter VII

Italian Lines

ITALIA LINE – LAURO LINES – SITMAR LINE – SIOSA LINE

ITALIA LINE (1932–)

FUNNEL – *White with green ring very close to narrow red top; black lip*

FLAG – *Red cross on white; white fleur-de-lys on red*

HULL – *Black with white riband after World War II until 1965 when changed to white with green riband (previously the colour of the South American ships only)*

Italy's status among the nations owning Western Ocean passenger tonnage has changed beyond recognition within the last half-century. Her first passenger liners comparable with those of North-West Europe did not appear until 1922, but in 1968 the Italia Line of Genoa became the principal operator of transatlantic passenger vessels in and out of New York.

In 1931 Italy possessed three important Western Ocean passenger lines. The Navigazione Generale Italiana of Genoa was the oldest and had two liners running to New York; the Lloyd Sabaudo, also of Genoa, was a newer company and possessed another two. Both had a single vessel approaching completion and much superior to their existing ships. The Cosulich Line of Trieste with a third pair of New York liners was rather the 'odd man out' and had been Austrian until the cession of Trieste to Italy in 1919. The first two companies served Genoa and Naples; the Cosulich, Adriatic ports (Yugoslav and Greek, as well as Italian). All three had South American passenger services in addition to their New York. North Atlantic receipts had been pooled since 1928 and arrangements made for the two big liners which were building to be placed in a seven-day Genoa–New York joint service.

As from 2 January 1932 the three companies were merged to

form the Italia Line (Italia–Flotte Riunite Cosulich–Lloyd Sabaudo–N.G.I.) of Genoa, although the Cosulich retained a measure of independence and a separate management at Trieste. The amalgamation was one of four made under government pressure to reduce competition between the various Italian shipping lines. A new arrangement dated 2 January 1937, carried fusion a stage further. The earlier amalgamations were reconstituted as subsidiaries of a single holding-company, Societa Finanziaria Marittima. The long-distance trades were divided between the Italia Line (Italia Societa di Navigazione) and the Lloyd Triestino, the former taking the Americas and the Triestino the rest of the world. Activities of the third and fourth subsidiaries were limited to the Mediterranean. The former Cosulich Line lost its semi-independence. The holding-company was regarded as a private one, although most of the capital came from a public body. The Italian Government subsidised some services, guaranteed a 4 per cent annual dividend and accepted responsibility for any financial deficits. Ships were declared interchangeable between the subsidiaries, though this provision has not affected any North Atlantic liners appearing in the fleet-list which follows. The general arrangements were re-affirmed in 1963, but the guarantees withdrawn.

On formation of the Italia Line the former 'N.G.I.' and Lloyd Sabaudo liner pairs continued running to New York, but when the new *Rex* and *Conte Di Savoia* commissioned during 1932 the Sabaudo ships were transferred to the Italia's River Plate service. Route of these Genoa vessels was by way of Naples and Gibraltar. *Rex* enabled her owners to claim the westbound Atlantic speed-record for two years. The ex-Cosulich *Saturnia* and *Vulcania* maintained their former itinerary from Trieste which included calls on either side of the Adriatic, at Sicilian and foreign ports and made them more dependent on emigrant traffic than the liners from Genoa. Social conditions in the Mediterranean have necessitated Italia vessels carrying more Classes of passenger than ships on the northern routes. For a time there was a Fourth Class, but this ceased during the 1930's.

World War II wiped out the Italia fleet, but restoration to Italy of *Saturnia* and her sister permitted resumption of Genoa–New York sailings in 1947 and new construction later allowed their return to the Trieste route. In 1964 two Italia liners were sailing from Genoa and two from Trieste and next year brought entry into service of *Michelangelo* and *Raffaelo*. These ships of 1965 took over the Genoa service and are the world's largest and fastest sisters. Their routeing to New York is via Cannes, Naples and Algeciras, and they sometimes visit other ports. The older ship displaced became responsible for the Trieste route and employment of the newer mainly cruising. The Trieste service is continued largely for political reasons and carries a heavy subsidy. Usual outward calls are Venice, Piraeus, Messina, Palermo, Naples, Algeciras and Halifax. Boston is substituted for Halifax on the homeward run from New York. Calls which the earlier ships made at Patras, Barcelona and Lisbon have been dropped, as also the pre-war Dubrovnik. Algeciras took the place of Gibraltar on both routes in mid–1967. A salient Italia Line feature is maintenance of almost the same frequency of New York sailings during the first three months as over the rest of the year. January–March departures for New York in 1969 totalled eight, against the four scheduled for all the non-Mediterranean passenger companies combined (including one by *Queen Elizabeth 2* which was cancelled).

The two finest passenger liners now sailing between Europe and the River Plate belong to the Italia company and the only passenger ships (other than 'Twelves') from Europe to the Pacific Coast of South America are another three of the Italia. Four 'Twelves' proceed through the Panama Canal as far north as Vancouver. Four exclusively cargo vessels complete the Italia fleet.

[241] *ROMA* ('26) 1932–40 Genoa
32,600t. 666 × 83 2–2 GT–4 20k.

Originally four Classes, later 537 First, 548 Second, 708 Third Class. *Roma* was withdrawn from service in 1939 with a view to re-engining and raising speed. The Italian Navy took possession of her for conversion at Genoa to the 30-knot aircraft-carrier *Aquila*. The work was approaching completion in 1943, but then ceased and the ship afterwards damaged by bombing. She was broken up, 1950.

[242] *AUGUSTUS* ('27) 1932–40 Genoa
30,400t. 666 × 83 2–2 M–4 19k.

Largest motorship in the world. Except for means of propulsion *Augustus* was virtually a sister of *Roma*. Funnels were of the steamship-type and both operative. In 1939 *Augustus* was taken in hand for re-engining with geared turbines. Later the Italian Navy decided to make her the aircraft-carrier *Sparviero*, but conversion had made little progress when the Germans scuttled the ship at Genoa. The hull was salved and scrapped in 1951.

[243]	*SATURNIA* ('27)	1932–43, 1947–65	Monfalcone
[244]	*VULCANIA* ('28)	1932–43, 1947–65	

23,950t. 601 × 80 1–2 M–2 18½k.

Former Cosulich liners, berthing 1700 travellers in four Classes and based on Trieste. Both ships were given new diesel machinery in 1935. Speed was improved by about 2 knots and tonnage became 24,450. Squat funnels of unusual width were reduced in size and a cowl with sloping top added in the case of *Saturnia*.

The United States commandeered these vessels after the Italian surrender. *Saturnia* became the hospital ship *Frances Y. Slanger* and *Vulcania* a troop transport without change of name. They were returned to Italy and *Vulcania* took the first post-war Italia sailing for New York, 20 Jan. 1947, from Genoa. Her sister followed in August. Trieste again became their base in October 1955. Post-war accommodation was 240 First, 270 Second and 860 Tourist Class. Final voyages were in March–April 1965. *Saturnia* went to shipbreakers, but the Siosa Line bought *Vulcania* and re-registered her as *Caribia*.

[245] *REX* 1932–44 Genoa

51,050t. 834 × 97 2–2 GT–4 27½k.

Ordered by the Navigazione Generale Italiana. Maiden voyage of *Rex* (400 First, 250 Second, 300 Tourist, 1300 Third) began at Genoa, 27 Sept. 1932, and was marred by a machinery defect which caused a long delay at Gibraltar. *Rex* is listed among the record-breakers because of a 4d. 13h. 58m. passage from Tarifa Point to the Ambrose (28·92 knots) the following August. She accomplished no outstanding crossing in the opposite direction and weather conditions made her route easier than the northern one associated with other record-breakers.

Rex was laid up in October 1939. British aircraft located the ship at anchor off Capo d'Istria and sank her by bombing.

[246] *CONTE DI SAVOIA* 1932–43 Monfalcone

48,500t. 786 × 96 2–2 GT–4 26½k.

The Lloyd Sabaudo's equivalent to *Rex* and laid down five months later. *Conte Di Savoia* was the smaller vessel and her best Tarifa–Ambrose crossing averaged only 27·53 knots. The name originally allocated was *Conte Azzuro*. General profile was not unlike *Rex*, but she had a cruiser-stern and the larger ship one of the counter-type. *Conte Di Savoia*'s claim to distinction was the installation of three Sperry stabilizers which were said to reduce rolling to 2½° in the worst of weather. She carried 343 First Class, 362 Second, 412 Tourist and 920 Third, and took her first sailing for New York on 30 Nov. 1932.

At commencement of the 1939–45 War *Conte Di Savoia* was laid up and in 1943 used as a troopship. British bombers set her on fire near Venice, 11 Sept. that year and she afterwards sank in shallow water. *Conte Di Savoia* was raised in 1945 but found beyond economic repair.

[247] *CONTE BIANCAMANO* ('25) 1950–56 Beardmore
24,400t. 626 × 76 2–2 GT–2 19k.

A former Lloyd Sabaudo ship and the last Italian liner ordered from a British yard. Transferred to South American service on completion of *Rex* and seized by the United States at Colon, March 1941. *Conte Biancamano* became the troopship *Hermitage*, was eventually restored to Italy and recovered her old name. *Conte Biancamano* (215 First, 333 Second, 950 Tourist) ran to New York from 1950 until 1956. Scrapped, 1960.

[248] *ANDREA DORIA* 1953–56 } Genoa
[249] *CRISTOFORO COLOMBO* 1954– }
29,100t. 627 × 90 1–1 GT–2 23k.

Andrea Doria and her sister (300 First, 244 Second and 703 Tourist) cleared Genoa on their maiden voyages in January 1953 and July 1954. *Cristoforo Colombo* was first to have been called *Duilo*.

An hour before midnight on 25 July 1956 the eastbound *Stockholm* [326] struck the westbound *Andrea Doria* about 25 miles west of Nantucket. Both ships were travelling fast, the Italian in fog and the Swede in the clear until immediately before the impact. An enormous hole was torn in *Andrea Doria*'s starboard side and the ship at once took a heavy list which made launching the port boats impossible. *Stockholm* was out of sight and incapacitated owing to the anchor chains having dropped through the damaged bow and held her to the bottom. Distress signals quickly brought two ships on the scene and *Ile De France* [142] responded to a special call for a liner with many lifeboats. *Andrea Doria* foundered eleven hours after the collision. Precise figures are disputed, but 52 out of the 1706 passengers and crew appear to have lost their lives. Legal proceedings to establish blame were eventually dropped by mutual consent.

Cristoforo Colombo has sailed in the Trieste service since the summer of 1965.

[250] *GIULIO CESARE* ('51) 1956–60 Monfalcone
[251] *AUGUSTUS* ('52) 1957–61 Trieste
27,100t. 618 × 88 1–1 M–2 21k.

First post-war Italia passenger liners. They belong to the Plate service, but *Giulio Cesare* (178 First, 288 Second, 714 Tourist) was moved to the New York as temporary replacement for *Andrea Doria* and *Augustus* joined her the following February. Both kept the white hulls of South American ships. Completion of *Leonardo Da Vinci* enabled *Giulio Cesare* to return to the Plate trade, but *Augustus* ran to New York most of 1961 and made two New York voyages the next summer.

[252] *LEONARDO DA VINCI* 1960– Genoa
33,400t. 675 × 92 1–1 GT–2 23k.

413 First Class, 342 Second and 571 Tourist. *Leonardo Da Vinci* is an improved and enlarged version of *Andrea Doria.* Maiden voyage began 30 June

1960. She was adapted for short-distance cruising in 1965–66 and has since used Naples as her base-port. Employment now alternates between Naples–Genoa–New York voyages (usually with Palermo, Barcelona and Lisbon calls) and short-distance cruises from New York.

[253]	*MICHELANGELO*	1965–	Genoa
[254]	*RAFFAELLO*	1965–	Trieste

45,900t. 801 × 102 2–2 GT–2 26½k.

The most noteworthy pair of sisters built for any shipping company since *Bremen* and *Europa* of 1929–30' They were five years under construction and the design repeatedly changed. Orders first placed were for smaller and slower ships after the style of *Leonardo Da Vinci*. Cost is believed to be about £20 million each. The yards where built and the Italia Line ultimately belongs to a gigantic state enterprise, the Institute of National Reconstruction and it is probably correct to say that construction of *Michelangelo* and *Raffaello* has been financed by the state. They are the only Atlantic liners built since *France* [148] which cannot be described as dual-purpose ships.

Numbers of passengers carried total 535 First, 550 Second and 690 Tourist. Internal decorations differ, but the liners are identical in other respects. The stem has a very pronounced rake which results in a length of 902 feet overall. Machinery is sited further aft than usual. *Raffaello* made 29¾ knots on her trials. The funnels provide these ships' most striking feature and represent one of the many ideas for minimising the smoke fall-out on deck. The funnels proper are of relatively small diameter and encased in lattice-work structures.

Michelangelo began with a short cruise from Genoa and took her initial New York departure, 12 May 1965. *Raffaello* followed on 25 July. Best crossings were made in 1966 from New York to Tarifa—*Michelangelo* at 27·21 knots and *Raffaello* at 27·15. Each vessel had the misfortune to make news during the first year's service. Complications arising from a fire on board *Raffaello* when 1800 miles short of New York on 31 Oct. 1965 put one propeller out of action and reduced speed to 12 knots. As she was running into a storm it was decided to return to Genoa and partial repairs brought speed up to 17 knots the following day. *Michelangelo*'s misfortune also occurred on an outward passage. The fore-superstructure was battered almost beyond recognition in a violent gale, 12 April 1966. Two passengers were killed, and another four, and seven of the crew, injured.

LAURO LINES (1953–1956)

FUNNEL – *Blue with white star and narrow black top*

FLAG – *On a blue burgee, a white star*

HULL – *White with narrow blue riband and blue waterline*

Lauro Lines (also known as Flotta Lauro) of Naples own a

considerable fleet and trade principally with Australia. One vessel, *Roma*, however, was diverted to make regular Naples–Genoa–Barcelona–Gibraltar–Halifax (outward)–New York voyages between May 1953 and the end of 1956. *Sydney*, her sister ship, made four Liverpool–Quebec voyages in 1953.

[256]	*ROMA* ('43)	1953–56	Tacoma, Wash.
[257]	*SYDNEY* ('44)	1953	San Francisco

14,700t. 465 × 70 1–1 GT–1 17k.

94 passengers in a cheap First Class and 708 inexpensive Tourist. *Roma* and *Sydney* were laid down as freighters, but converted to escort-carriers and served in the British Navy as *Atheling* and *Fencer*.

SITMAR LINE (1953–1957)

FUNNEL – *Yellow with large blue 'V'*

FLAG – *On blue, a large white 'V'*

HULL – *White with green waterline*

Initial letters of the owning company, the Societa Italiana Trasporti Marittimi, provide a name for the Sitmar Line which resembles the Lauro in employing second-hand tonnage in the emigrant trades, mainly the Australian. Transatlantic voyages, summer only, which began in 1953 and lasted until 1957 were mostly from Bremerhaven to the St. Lawrence whereas the Lauro's were Italy–New York. *Fairsea* made four to Canada in 1953 and these were augmented by two by the ex-'Victory' ship *Castel Bianco*. *Castel Felice* took over the following summer. Fares roughly corresponded with the Lauro. Voyages commenced at Bremerhaven with the majority to Quebec and/or Montreal and frequent Rotterdam, Havre and Southampton calls, but some were to New York. *Fairsea* took three special Greenock–Quebec sailings in 1957. Final departure was to New York, September 1957. Five *Castel Felice* Amsterdam–Havre–Southampton–New York sailings were announced for 1966, but cancelled.

Sitmar headquarters, originally in Genoa, have latterly been transferred to Naples. Newest additions to the fleet are registered in Liberia, although Panama was used for a short while.

[261] *FAIRSEA* ('41) 1953, 1957 11,850t. 465 × 70 1–1 M–1 16½k.

Tourist Class only, mainly 'dormitory'. Previously the American-built British escort-carrier *Charger*.

[262] *CASTEL FELICE* ('30) 1954–57 Stephen
12,150t. 470 × 64 1–1 GT–2 16½k.

Originally the British India's *Keren* and underwent several changes of name. Completely reconstructed at Genoa. Accommodation for 596 Tourist Class in cabins and 944 in 'dormitories' was altered to 28 in a cheap First and 1173 Tourist in 1954–55.

SIOSA LINE (1957, 1959–1960)

FUNNEL – *Blue with white device of the house-flag and narrow black top*

FLAG – *On a blue burgee, a large white 'S' enclosed in white oval frame*

HULL – Ascania, *white*

Until 1961 the Siosa Line formed part of a dual-organisation called the Grimaldi Siosa Lines which began as the Grimaldi of Genoa. Sicilian registration brought financial advantages from the Italian Government and a second company, the Sicula Oceanica of Palermo, was formed and termed the Siosa Line. Grimaldi and Siosa ships had different house-flags and funnels, and ran side-by-side until the last Grimaldi vessel was sold. Main Siosa services are Italy–West Indies and Southampton–West Indies, but there have been some emigrant round-voyages to the St. Lawrence. Tonnage employed was second-hand with similar style accommodation to the Lauro and Sitmar Lines. Sailings by *Ascania* were Southampton–Havre–Quebec; by *Irpinia*, Palermo–Naples–Genoa–Quebec–Montreal. The only Canadian round-voyages were in 1957 and 1959–60, but there were also a few crossings from Southampton to Canada or New York around these years, returning via the West Indies.

[266] *ASCANIA* ('26) 1957 9550t. 471 × 60 1–2 GT–2 14½k.

Previously *Florida* of the Société Générale de Transports Maritimes.

[267] *IRPINIA* ('29) 1959–60 12,300t. 510 × 67 2–2 GT–2 14½k.

Ex-*Campana* and bought from the same owners as *Ascania*. 120 cheap First Class and 1040 Tourist. *Irpinia* was converted to a motorship in 1962 and much improved.

CHAPTER VIII

Spanish and Various Eastern Mediterranean Lines

COMPAÑIA TRASATLANTICA ESPAÑOLA – CHANDRIS LINES – YUGOSLAV LINE – UNITED ARAB MARITIME COMPANY – KHEDIVIAL MAIL LINE – ZIM LINES

(For Greek Line and Home Lines *see* Chapter VI)

COMPAÑIA TRASATLANTICA ESPAÑOLA (–)

Spanish

FUNNEL – *Black*

FLAG – *On blue, a large white ball*

Mainstream of North-West Europe's westbound steamships has always been to the Newfoundland Banks and there dispersed for temperate ports, but the principal New World interests of Spain and Portugal continue to lie in Latin America. Iberian shipping lines carry passengers to the United States only via Spanish-speaking ports and their inclusion among the North Atlantic companies is questionable. The Portuguese representative, the Companhia Colonial de Navegaçao, extended its Caribbean service to Miami in October 1956, but the 21,000-ton *Santa Maria* proceeds as far south as Venezuela before turning northwards and through-passengers from Lisbon to the United States are few. The Compañia Trasatlantica Española is another matter, for it reaches New York via Mexico and now returns direct to Spain. Passages to and from New York were more indirect in the past and no year from which the company can fairly be regarded as a North Atlantic passenger-carrier can be given.

The Compañia Trasatlantica was a reconstruction of an earlier concern and registered at Barcelona in 1881. The steamers traded to the Caribbean islands and adjacent mainland, though New York appeared as an off-shoot from the Cuba–Mexico service in 1886. New York became more conspicuous in the sailing lists at the beginning of the 1914–18 War, though still treated as rather an incidental call for the ships working from Barcelona to Havana and Vera Cruz. As the war progressed the company came to identify itself more with Spanish northern ports than Barcelona. Administration was moved to Madrid in 1938 and the amplified title, Compañia Trasatlantica Española, adopted. The Spanish Civil War had disrupted the company's activities and the most suitable point for accepting the line as a passenger carrier between Europe and New York is probably late 1939 when regular sailings were resumed with Biscay ports substituted for Barcelona. Normal routeing today is Bilbao–Santander–Gijon–Vigo–San Juan–Vera Cruz – New York – Corunna – Gijon – Santander – Bilbao. San Juan, Puerto Rico, replaced the old Havana call in 1963 and there have been many other variations. A few voyages exclude San Juan and Vera Cruz, but add Lisbon westbound. Fares are less than from Spanish Mediterranean ports by the Italian or Greek lines.

The company operates two more southerly passenger services, one from Southampton via North Spanish ports and the other from Genoa by way of Barcelona, Cadiz, etc. Both are to the West Indies and the Caribbean mainland.

[271] *MARQUES DE COMILLAS* ('28) 1939–53 Ferrol
[272] *MAGALLANES* ('28) 1940–53 Cadiz
9900t. 460 × 56 1–2 GT–2 16k.

155 First Class, 82 Second and 342 Third. Dates shown are the years these ships resumed New York sailings after the Spanish Civil War, but they had certainly visited New York earlier. Civil War employment was fetching munitions from Odessa. Both were transferred to other services in 1953. *Magallanes* went to breakers four years later and her sister was destroyed by fire at Ferrol, 1961.

[273] *HABANA* ('23) 1940–? Bilbao
10,550t. 480 × 61 1–2 GT–2 16k.

Formerly called *Alfonso XIII,* this vessel was renamed *Habana* in 1931. Twelve years later she was reconstructed after a fire at New York and passenger accommodation reduced to 112 First Class only. *Habana* had left the service to New York by 1950 and was sold in 1961.

[274]	*GUADALUPE*	1953–	Bilbao
[275]	*COVADONGA*	1953–	Bilbao

10,250t. 457 × 62 1–1 M–1 16½k.

Typical squat-funnelled motor vessels laid down for another company as the cargo ships *Monasterio De Guadalupe* and *Monasterio De La Rabida.* The Compañia Trasatlantica bought them after launching, altered the names and fitted 105 First Class and 245 Tourist berths.

CHANDRIS LINES (1966–) *Greek*

FUNNEL – *Light blue with large white 'X' close to narrow black top*

FLAG – *Light blue, white letter and stripes*

HULL – *White with black waterline*

Several one-ship companies operate under the general name, Chandris Lines. All began in the 1960's and most work between Europe and the Antipodes. Piraeus is the home-port. They belong to Anthony J. Chandris and the 'X' of the flag and funnel is the Greek equivalent of 'CH'. Newest of the Chandris Lines is the former Greek subsidiary of Home Lines (*see* page 143), bought at the end of 1965. Name of the Home subsidiary company (National Hellenic American Line) was kept to designate this particular service and *Vasilissa Freideriki* continued running on her existing Mediterranean–New York route. A much newer vessel, *Amerikanis*, replaced her after two years and the route was extended and modified to become Haifa – Limasol (westward) – Piraeus – Messina (westward) – Naples – Lisbon – Halifax (westward) – New York. Haifa and Limasol are sometimes omitted. Employment during the winter months consists of short cruises from New York.

	VASILLISSA FREIDERIKI	1966–67	*See ATLANTIC* [226]
[276]	*AMERIKANIS* ('52)	1968–	Belfast

20,400t. 541 × 74 1–2 GT–2 17½k.

Amerikanis (860 passengers in First and Tourist Classes) is the former Union-Castle *Kenya Castle*. Very extensive reconstruction has increased former tonnage considerably. The name signifies, 'American Lady'.

YUGOSLAV LINE (1949–) *Yugoslav*

FUNNEL – *Blue with narrow black top, a narrow blue band and a broad white bearing a red star*

FLAG – *On blue, a white diamond (corners touching edges of flag) with red star in centre*

HULL – *Grey with white line, but the ships of* 1965/66 *are deep cream with blue line. Waterline, green in both cases. Since about 1960 'Jugolinija' has been painted on either side in white or blue as appropriate.*

The Yugoslav Line (Jugolavenska Linijska Plovidba) of Rijeka began in 1947 and maintains many cargo services. In the autumn of 1949 two vessels with limited passenger accommodation entered the Rijeka–New York trade and were supplemented by three 'Twelves'. Four sisterships of good speed took their places in 1965–66. The present route is basically Rijeka–Naples–Genoa–Casablanca–New York, continuing to Philadelphia and calling at Venice (westbound) and Trieste (homeward). Other ports are frequently added. Two grades of passenger are carried at fares which are best described as Tourist Class and a Cheap Tourist.

[281] *HRVATSKA* ('45) 1949–65 7900t. 437 × 62 1–2 GT–1 16k.

Originally *St. Lawrence Victory*, beached at Korcula in 1947 after being mined but bought, repaired and renamed *Zagreb* by the Yugoslav Line. Renamed a second time and fitted with 60 passenger berths.

[282] *SRBIJA* 1949–65 6650t. 440 × 60 1–2 M–1 15k.

Hull built in Germany but assigned to Yugoslavia as reparations and completed in Holland, 1949, as the 'Twelve' *Drvar*. Accommodation was soon increased to 44 berths and name changed to *Srbija*.

[283] *VISEVICA* 1965–
[284] *TUHOBIC* 1965–
[285] *KLEK* 1965–
[286] *ZVIR* 1966–
} 7750t. 443 × 67 1–1 M–1 18k

20 passengers in the first grade and 30 in the second. Funnel and upperworks are a long way aft and the mast is a short structure immediately before the funnel. Built at Rijeka.

UNITED ARAB MARITIME COMPANY (1962–)

Egyptian

FUNNEL – *Blue with large white ball bearing eagle of the house-flag; narrow black top*

FLAG – *Blue pennant with large gold eagle standing on two hemipheres (blue and white); the body, a red-white-black shield divided vertically with two green stars on the white*

HULL – *Grey with green waterline*

The entire seagoing merchant fleet of Egypt (otherwise called the United Arab Republic) belongs to and is operated by the state-owned United Arab Maritime Company which came into being in 1962. Services include one from Alexandria to Toronto and the ships carry a limited number of passengers at Tourist Class rates as far as Montreal. Ports of call along the route are Beirut, Piraeus, Genoa, Barcelona, Lisbon and Quebec. There are occasional winter sailings to St. John via Halifax, but the United Arab transatlantic service is at present suspended.

This Egyptian passenger service to Canada is a direct continuation of an earlier one which commenced in 1954 and belonged to the Alexandria Navigation Company. *Star of Assuan* and *Port Said*, the vessels employed, may well have been 'Twelves' in the 1950's. Late in 1959 the Alexandria Navigation and another company were taken over by a new concern, the Société Générale pour la Navigation Maritime, although it seems to have kept its separate identity. The Khedivial Mail Line was amalgamated with the Société in July 1961. The Société itself remains something of a mystery, but changed its name to the United Arab Maritime Company the following year when the components were welded into a single state-owned fleet.

[291] *STAR OF ASSUAN* ('48) 1962–64 5450t. 376 × 55 1–2 M–1 13½k.
40 passengers. Moved to North European service.

[292] *PORT SAID* ('49) 1962 }
[293] *STAR OF SUEZ* ('48) 1964– } 6450t. 380 × 57 1–2 M–1 14k.

Built at Trieste and berthing 40 passengers. *Port Said* was transferred to the North European service on relief by *Cleopatra*.

SALAH EL DIN 1961–63; *CLEOPATRA* 1962– *See MOHAMED ALI EL KEBIR* [297] and *KHEDIVE ISMAIL* [296]

KHEDIVIAL MAIL LINE (1948–1956) *Egyptian*

FUNNEL – (a) *Green with white crescent and three stars; black top*

(b) *1952. White with white-red-white-black bands under black top*

FLAG – *White inscribed 'Khedivial Mail Line' in red Arabic characters; wide red border with small white crescent and star in each corner*

The Khedivial Mail Line, previously British, became an Egyptian concern in 1937. Trading sphere was originally the Eastern Mediterranean and Red Sea, but *Khedive Ismail* opened an Alexandria–New York service on 15 March 1948 and a sistership followed soon afterwards. The itinerary varied, though Beirut, Naples, Genoa and Marseilles were the usual calls and the ships continued from New York to Philadelphia. In 1954–55 a third vessel, *Gumhuryat Misr* (the former British *Lady Nelson*), made two or three voyages along the route. Regular departures ended after the British-French attack on the Suez Canal, 1956, although a few stray voyages took place later. The Khedivial Mail was amalgamated in mid-1961 with the Societé Générale pour la Navigation Maritime (later the United Arab Company).

[296]	*KHEDIVE ISMAIL* ('44)	1948–56	
	U. Arab *CLEOPATRA*	1962–	8200t. 437 × 62
[297]	*MOHAMED ALI EL KEBIR* ('44)	1948–56	1–2 GT–1 16k.
	U. Arab *SALAH EL DIN*	1961–63	

Ex-'Victory' ships built on the Pacific Coast, *United Victory* and *Atchison Victory*. 77 passengers. The original fare charged corresponded with Second Class, but had become a Tourist Class rate by the 1960's.

The Khedivial Mail transferred both vessels to a European service, and re-named the first *Cleopatra* in 1956. Name of the second was changed four years afterwards. *Salah El Din* caught fire in Canada, was badly damaged and sold to become the Liberian *Mercantile Victory*.

ZIM LINES (1953–1967) *Israeli*

FUNNEL – *White with seven gold stars between two narrow blue bands (as house-flag)*

FLAG – *White with light blue stripes and gold stars*

HULL – Israel *and later ships, white with green waterline*

A major achievement of Israel has been creation of the Zim

Israel Navigation Company of Haifa, usually called briefly Zim Lines. About a third of the capital belongs to the Government of Israel and most of the balance to public bodies. The name, 'Zim', is derived from 'Zi Mischari', the Hebrew words for mercantile marine. The fleet began with a remarkably mixed collection of second-hand vessels, but now consists of some forty ships, all built since the mid-1960's and a few of them passenger-carriers.

Zim Lines held a place among the North Atlantic passenger companies for some years, although the Haifa–New York service has been limited to cargo since the autumn of 1967. Intermediate ports underwent many changes. Those of *Shalom* can perhaps be summarised as Naples or Genoa, Marseilles (Cannes in the final year) and Barcelona, Malaga or Lisbon. The earlier ships usually added Piraeus, Gibraltar and Funchal.

The pre-*Shalom* vessels provided only kosher meals. The more ambitious *Shalom* needed to book passengers from/to European ports as well as Haifa and was also intended for extensive pleasure-cruising. She was therefore built with two kitchens—kosher and non-kosher—but this commonsense arrangement caused trouble even before launching. The rigidly orthodox minority in Israel objected and possessed political power out of all proportion to their numerical strength. In order to avoid a political crisis the Government was ultimately compelled to yield and concede that the cuisine should be entirely kosher except when cruising from New York. The story is hardly credible and the result was a foregone conclusion. *Shalom* made only four transatlantic voyages a year, at the peak of each season, and was sold March 1967 after only three years' operation. She had cost over $20 million and fetched little more than $15 million. The older ships had been sold 12 months before and *Shalom* was delivered to the German Atlantic Line in November 1967.

	JERUSALEM	1953–55	*See BERGENSFJORD* [311]
[301]	*ISRAEL*	1955–66	Hamburg (Deutsche Werft)
[302]	*ZION*	1956–66	Hamburg (Deutsche Werft)

9850t. 455 × 65 1–2 GT–1 17½k.

Built under Israeli–German Reparations Agreement. *Israel*, first to have been named *Theodor Herzl*, commenced her maiden New York sailing, October 1955. Accommodation provided for 24 First Class, 179 Tourist in cabins and 120 in 'dormitories', although main source of revenue was cargo. The Empresa

Insulana de Navegaçao of Lisbon bought the pair and renamed them *Amgra Do Heroismo* and *Amelia De Mello* respectively.

[303] *JERUSALEM* ('57) 1958–64 9900t. 435 × 65 1–1 GT–2 18½k.

Built at Hamburg for the Zim Mediterranean service, but *Jerusalem* cruised from New York or Miami every winter from 1958–69 to 1963–64. This entailed transatlantic crossings from Haifa and she also made a Haifa–New York round-voyage at the height of each season. Late in 1966 the Peninsular & Occidental took *Jerusalem* on bare-boat charter and called her *Miami*. Two years later the Eastern Steamship Company bought the ship which is now *New Bahama Star* (Liberian flag) and has replaced the former *Arosa Star* [237].

[304] *SHALOM* 1964 St. Nazaire
Ger. Atl. *HANSEATIC* 1967–
25,300t. 555 × 81 2 (abreast)–1 GT–2 20k.

A French subsidy enabled the builders to win the contract to build *Shalom*. The two funnels abreast and very pronounced rake on the bow give this handsome ship a most distinctive appearance. The name, *Shalom*, means 'Peace'. *Shalom* was 75 per cent owned by the Israeli Governmnet and 25 per cent by Zim Lines. She began with a short European cruise and left Haifa on her maiden New York sailing, 17 April 1964. Extensive pleasure-cruising was always intended and occupied eight months each year. On 26 Nov. 1964 *Shalom* collided with the Norwegian tanker *Stolt Dagali* in fog, 40 miles south-east of New York. The tanker was cut in two and the after-part sank. Some small changes soon afterwards gave *Shalom* accommodation for 148 First and 864 Tourist Class. Accumulated losses during three years' operation are variously given as $13 million and $16 million. Zin Lines were only too pleased to accept the unexpected German offer to buy her to replace the former *Empress of Scotland* [51].

The first German sailing was on a cruise from Hamburg, 27 Dec. 1967. The ex-*Shalom* had been designed for the Mediterranean route to New York and unfortunately proved a poor seaboat in more northerly waters. After one season's transatlantic work as *Hanseatic* she was allocated to permanent cruising.

Chapter IX

Scandinavian and Baltic Lines

NORWEGIAN AMERICA LINE – SWEDISH AMERICAN LINE – POLISH OCEAN LINES (formerly GDYNIA–AMERICA LINE) – BALTIC STEAMSHIP COMPANY – EAST ASIATIC COMPANY

NORWEGIAN AMERICA LINE (1913–) *Norwegian*

FUNNEL – *Buff with red-white-blue-white-red bands (see* Bergensfjord *illustration on page 88)*

FLAG – *A burgee with horizontal stripes of red, white (double width) and red; blue letters 'N.A.L.' on the white*

HULL – *Silver-grey*

Dissolution of the Union with Sweden encouraged Norway to look across the Atlantic instead of eastwards and the Norwegian America Line (Norske Amerikalinje) was founded in 1910 with government assistance. The first of two passenger liners ordered in Britain, *Kristianafjord*, sailed for New York on 4 June 1913 and neutrality during the 1914–18 World War brought profits which quickly set the company on a firm basis. The Norwegian-America's first motor passenger ship commissioned in 1938 and the entire passenger fleet has been diesel-driven since 1965. Voyages begin at Oslo and usually include Copenhagen and Kristiansand, although one or other may be omitted. Some sailings are via Stavanger and Bergen. The line possesses a large freighter fleet.

The Norwegian American and the Swedish American passenger services to New York have a great deal in common. They are alike in having made the Danish capital a port of call since World War II and routeing their ships north of Scotland through Fair Island Channel. The companies working on more southern routes have been able to adopt safety-tracks which take eastbound vessels well to the south of Nantucket, but this is clearly impracticable for the Scandinavian. The Norwegians and Swedes are the only nations which have ordered really large motor liners in the 1960's. Pleasure-cruising from New York has been a major source of income for many years and all post-1945 ships except *Stockholm* [326], have been dual-purpose liners. Both lines abandoned winter trans-atlantic voyages in 1960–61 and departures for New York are now only four or five at the height of the season or in connection with cruises.

[311] *BERGENSFJORD* 1913–46 Birkenhead
Home *ARGENTINA* 1952
Zim *JERUSALEM* 1953–55
11,000t. 512 × 61 2–2 4E–2 17½k.

Bergensfjord's sister, *Kristianiafjord*, was wrecked near Cape Race, 15 July 1917. *Bergensfjord* herself underwent many changes, beginning with conversion from a coal-burner to oil when seven years old. In 1930–31 she was extensively refitted in Germany and given low-pressure turbines to augment the reciprocating machinery, thereby raising speed from 16 to 17½ knots. At end of the decade passenger complement had become 90 Cabin, 155 Tourist Class and 500 Third.

From April until November 1940 this ship was laid up at New York. She then steamed to Halifax and was converted to a troop transport. After hostilities *Bergensfjord* was reconditioned and made some more commercial voyages prior to sale to Home Lines, November 1946. The new owners renamed her *Argentina* for their South American trade, but her 1952 voyages were between Italy and New York. Resold in February 1953, she became *Jerusalem*, with 33 inexpensive First Class berths and 741 Tourist. Zim Lines made her interchangeable between their New York and Marseilles services. *Jerusalem* crossed the Atlantic for the last time in September 1955 and was scrapped in 1959 under the name *Aliya*.

[312] *STAVANGERFJORD* 1918–63 Birkenhead
13,150t. 531 × 64 2–2 4E2 17½k.

Two tall thin funnels gave *Stavangerfjord* a broad resemblance to *Bergensfjord*, though she had a cruiser-stern. She was laid down in 1915 to provide a three-ship service. The British Government ordered indefinite suspension of work but construction was resumed in 1917 by special arrangement and completed May 1918. Furnaces were altered from coal to oil-burning in 1923 and a 1931–32 refit wrought similar improvements to *Bergensfjord's*. Rating of accommodation was then 147 Cabin, 207 Tourist and 820 Third. In 1940 the Germans found *Stavangerfjord* at Oslo and used her for accommodating troops.

The Norwegian America's first post-war passenger sailing was taken by this ship, August 1945. *Stavangerfjord* lost her rudder in a gale 500 miles east of Newfoundland, 9 Dec. 1953, and hove-to for two days. An attempt to take her in tow failed, but the weather moderated and she resumed her passage home, steering with her screws. She carried 66 First Class passengers, 184 Second and 402 Tourist passengers in the final years. *Stavangerfjord* made her last departure from the Hudson on 3 Dec. 1963 and was sold immediately after arrival home. She had crossed the North Atlantic 770 times and no other Western Ocean passenger liner has served a single owner for so long.

[313] *OSLOFJORD* 1938–40 Bremen (Weser)
18,650t. 563 × 73 2–2 M–2 17½k.

The first *Oslofjord* was laid up at New York when Germany invaded Norway, but in November ordered to the United Kingdom for conversion to a troopship. She was damaged by an acoustic mine near the mouth of the Tyne, 13 Dec. 1940, and became a total loss.

[314] *OSLOFJORD* 1949– Amsterdam
16,850t. 519 × 72 1–2 M–2 20k.

179 First Class and 467 Tourist. *Oslofjord* left Oslo on her maiden voyage, 26 Nov. 1949. She has been used entirely for cruising from British ports since end of the 1967 Atlantic season.

[315] *BERGENSFJORD* 1956– Swan Hunter
18,750t. 518 × 72 1–2 M–2 20k.

Much the same as *Oslofjord*, although with a foot extra draught and accommodating 125 First and 750 Tourist Class.

[316] *SAGAFJORD* 1965– La Seyne
24,000t. 550 × 80 1–2 M–2 20k.

The La Seyne yard at Toulon won the building contract for *Sagafjord* with aid of a £1 million subsidy from the French Government. The ship is only 60 per cent owned by the Norwegian America Line and the balance by Leif Hoegh. Initial departure from Oslo for New York was 18 May 1965. *Sagafjord* carries 450 First Class passengers and 820 Tourist.

SWEDISH AMERICAN LINE (1915–) *Swedish*

FUNNEL – *Pale buff with ball-and-crowns device of the house-flag (see* Kungsholm *illustration on page 97)*

FLAG – *On white, three gold crowns inside a large blue ball*

HULL – *White*

The Swedes planned their North Atlantic passenger line shortly after their Norwegian neighbours, but war intervened before contracts for the appropriate ships had been placed. They were fortunate in being able to buy an elderly Holland-America liner which was renamed *Stockholm* and despatched on her maiden New

York voyage, 11 December 1915. It was not until late 1925 that the Swedish American Line obtained a passenger vessel direct from the builder—*Gripsholm*, notable on account of being the earliest Western Ocean diesel-driven passenger ship. Prior to this the company had to buy second-hand steamers or charter. The delay in securing newly-built tonnage brought the compensation that the Swedish vessels outclassed their Norwegian rivals during the 1930's.

The Swedish American Line (Svenska Amerika Linien) is based on Gothenburg and belongs to the Broström Combine. Copenhagen is now the only call made by the passenger liners on their way to and from New York, and often omitted. Pleasure-cruising has become a leading activity and further information will be found in the Norwegian America Sub-Chapter. An interesting feature of this company is that disposal of passenger ships has always been to other operators.

The Swedish American Company has been conspicuous in the part played in the post-war creation and resurrection of other Western Ocean passenger lines as can be seen in the Home Lines and Norddeutscher Lloyd Sub-Chapters. Again, in 1955 the Swedish American provided 45 per cent of the capital for a new Danish line, to be called the Denmark-America, but the idea fizzled out.

Sweden's North Atlantic passenger concern owns a number of cargo ships and is a member of the Atlantic Container Lines consortium.

[321]	*DROTTNINGHOLM* ('05)	1920–48	Stephen
	Home *BRASIL*	1950	
	Home *HOMELAND*	1951–54	

11,200t. 520 × 60 1–2 T–3 15½k.

Drottningholm saw even lengthier service than *Stavangerfjord*, but had four different owners and spent a brief period away from the North Atlantic. She began as the Allan *Virginian* and was completed a few weeks after her sister, *Victorian*, the pioneer turbine-driven ocean liner. *Virginian* passed to the Canadian Pacific while under requisition as an armed merchant cruiser and was sold to the Swedish–American Line on release. Maiden voyage as *Drottningholm* commenced in May 1920.

In 1922 *Drottningholm* was re-engined in Sweden with geared turbines and converted to an oil-burner. An original speed of 17½ knots had fallen away badly, but this rejuvenation restored a comfortable 16. Destruction of *Stockholm* [324] which should have relieved her, gave the ex-Allan veteran a fresh lease of life. World War II employment was on behalf of the International Red Cross and in March 1946 she took the first post-war Europe–New York passenger sailing of any company.

Home Lines took possession of *Drottningholm* in mid-1948 and registered her as *Brasil* for their South American trade. She carried out some Naples–New York voyages in 1950. Renamed *Homeland*, this ship opened the Hamburg–Southampton–Cherbourg–Halifax (westbound)–New York service on 16 June 1951 and then berthed 85 First Class and 866 Tourist passengers. From the following spring until the end of 1954 *Homeland* was based on Genoa and routed to New York via Naples.

[322] *GRIPSHOLM* 1925 Tyne (Vickers)
Nord. Ll. *GRIPSHOLM* 1954
Nord. Ll. *BERLIN* 1955–66
17,950t. 550 × 74 2–2 M–2 16k.

The North Atlantic's first motor liner and an entirely successful one. *Gripsholm* (127 First, 482 Second, 948 Third) looked like a steam vessel and, unlike later motorships, both funnels were effective. Wartime employment resembled *Drottningholm*'s. She received a new bow and shorter though wider funnels in 1949–50 and passenger accommodation was changed to 98 First Class and 878 Tourist. *Gripsholm* rescued 45 men from the burning Norwegian freighter *Black Hawk*, 18 July 1952, 75 miles from New York.

Gripsholm was transferred to the Norddeutscher Lloyd and her departure from Bremerhaven on 1 Feb. 1954 was the first New York passenger sailing under the German flag since 1939, although all the 1954 voyages commenced at Gothenburg and were made via Bremerhaven. *Berlin* supplanted the Swedish name the following January. Gross tonnage then amounted to 18,600. The Swedish American Line retained half-ownership of *Berlin* until the beginning of 1959. Normal routeing was directly from Bremerhaven to New York, but often included Southampton in either direction during the height of the summer season. From 1964 *Berlin* was the oldest transatlantic passenger ship remaining operative and she cruised extensively. Final departure from New York was 3 Sept. 1966 and she went to shipbreakers shortly after arrival back at Bremerhaven.

[323] *KUNGSHOLM* 1928–42 Hamburg (Blohm & Voss)
Home *ITALIA* 1949–64
20,050t. 582 × 78 2–2 M–2 17k.

Another motor vessel with a steamship profile. Original passenger capacity was much the same as *Gripsholm*. *Kungsholm* escaped with light damage after colliding with the tanker *A. G. Bedford* off Nantucket, 1937. Employment in 1940–41 was cruising to the West Indies from New York, but the United States planned to commandeer the ship. The Swedes therefore agreed to sell *Kungsholm* in January 1942 and the Americans fitted her out as the troopship *John Ericsson*. The original owners repurchased her, July 1947, after serious damage by fire at New York, but at once resold her to Home Lines.

Home Lines registered the ship as *Italia* for their South American trade. A Genoa refit altered accommodation to 120 First and 1320 Tourist Class on a gross tonnage of 21,500. During June 1949 *Italia* was moved to the Genoa–Lisbon–New York route and in March 1952 placed in the Hamburg service to New York. In 1959–60 she ran from Hamburg to Montreal instead of the Hudson. Home Lines sold *Italia* for use as a floating hotel at Freetown, Bahamas, in the 1964 spring, but the venture failed and she was sold for breaking up the following year.

[324] (*STOCKHOLM* Launched 1938) } Monfalcone
[325] (*STOCKHOLM* Launched 1940) }
28,000t. 642 × 83 2–2* M–3 18½k.

Drottningholm had entered her fourth decade and outlasted all her Western Ocean contemporaries before a replacement was ordered. Her successor would have been larger than any Swedish American liner before or since, but neither she nor a duplicate was ever to join the company's fleet. The first was destroyed by fire in December 1938 while fitting out. The name *Stockholm* was transferred to a replica which was laid down. This second vessel was commandeered to become the Italian troopship *Sabaudia* and sunk by aerial bombing at Trieste on 7 July 1944.

[326] *STOCKHOLM* 1948–49 Gothenburg
11,700t. 481 × 69 1–1 M–2 18½k.

For the third attempt to replace the veteran *Drottningholm* the Swedish American Line was compelled to build in Sweden and accept a ship of relatively small dimensions. *Stockholm* started with a complement of 113 First and 282 Tourist Class passengers, but this was altered to 24 First and 548 Tourist after seven years.

See under *Andrea Doria* [248] for the ramming and sinking of that Italian liner. The impact telescoped 60 feet of *Stockholm*'s bow and the effect would have been worse if her stem had not had such a pronounced rake. Of her crew, 3 lost their lives and 4 were seriously injured. The Swedish ship afterwards carried 545 survivors to New York and spent six months under repair at New York. *Stockholm* was sold in January 1960 to become an East German workers' cruising-liner *Völkerfreundshaft*.

[327] *KUNGSHOLM* 1953 Flushing
Nord. Ll. *EUROPA* 1966–
22,050t. 530 × 77 2–2* M–2 19k.

Kungsholm (132 First, 637 Tourist) was the biggest motor liner afloat when new and opened her career with a New York sailing in Nobember 1953. The Norddeutscher Lloyd bought the ship, September 1965, as consort for *Bremen* [287], although maiden departure from Bremerhaven did not take place until the next year.

[328] *GRIPSHOLM* 1957– Genoa

23,200t. 551 × 82 2–2* M–2 19k.

A larger version of *Kungsholm* [327]. The second *Gripsholm* has berths for 150 First Class and 612 Tourist travellers. In November 1967 an engine-room explosion disabled her off Newfoundland. She remained stopped for eight hours and then managed to continue to New York on her port engine at 10 knots.

[329] *KUNGSHOLM* 1966– Brown

26,700t. 570 × 87 2–2* M–2 21k.

160 First, 606 Tourist. The present *Kungsholm*, a marked improvement on earlier tonnage, is the largest and most powerful motor liner in the world. She was built under a 'build-and-sell' policy, framed to keep the Swedish American passenger fleet absolutely up-to-date. Completion was delayed three months and the builders sustained heavy financial loss. *Kungsholm* relieved her 1953 namesake and allocation of the identical name is explained by a desire to avoid *Stockholm* with its unfortunate associations.

POLISH OCEAN LINES (formerly GDYNIA-AMERICA LINE)

(1935–1951, 1957–) *Polish*

FUNNEL – *Yellow with red band, edged with white and interrupted by shield-and-trident device of the house-flag*

FLAG – (a) *As 1961, but with lettering 'GAL' instead of 'PLO'.*

(b) *1961. White with red stripe; white-and-red device*

HULL – *Black and white riband.*

Until 1951 Polish Ocean Lines (Polskie Linje Oceanicze) were known as the Gdynia-America Shipping Line and the North Atlantic service is still often referred to by that name. They are owned by the Polish Government. Association with the East Asiatic Company of Copenhagen has always been close and Polish Ocean ancestry can be traced back to the Russian American Line, an East Asiatic subsidiary which started operations in 1906 and ceased during World War I. In 1921 the line was re-created under the Danish flag as the Baltic American, working from Ventspils with ships which were almost exclusively emigrant-carriers. After nine years the Baltic American Line was sold to the Poles and renamed the Polish Transatlantic Shipping Company. The first of two large motor vessels joined the fleet in 1935 and the name,

Gdynia-America, then adopted, together with the route Gdynia–Copenhagen–Halifax–New York. The new ships were unusual in having their best accommodation rated Tourist Class, a grading explained by the primary need to cater for emigrants.

Nazi occupation of Poland caused suspension of operations, but these were resumed in May 1947. A Southampton call was introduced and Halifax dropped. Later in the year the Gdynia-America opened a subsidiary passenger service, Italy–New York, though this did not last. After *Batory*'s January 1951 voyage the New York harbour authorities refused the Poles further use of a pier for political reasons and this ended sailings to the United States. August 1957 brought a return to the North Atlantic with Canadian ports substituted for New York. The renewed service was to Quebec and Montreal during the months the St. Lawrence is open and to Halifax from December to March, but winter voyages have been replaced by cruising from European ports since 1960–61. The Copenhagen call remains, but Southampton was often omitted until *Stefan Batory* opened the 1969 season with Southampton as her homeward British call and London her westbound.

[331] *PILSUDSKI* 1935–39 } Monfalcone
[332] *BATORY* 1936–51, 1957– }
14,300t. 499 × 71 2–2* M–2 17½k.

355 Tourist, 404 Third Class. *Pilsudski*, converted to an armed merchant cruiser, was sunk by submarine off the Humber, 26 Nov. 1939. *Batory* escaped from Gdynia to Sweden when the Nazi hordes overran Poland and became a troopship.

Batory ran in the Bombay trade after termination of the New York service. Passenger quarters were remodelled to take 76 First and 740 Tourist Class before she returned to the Atlantic in 1957. Transatlantic work ended in 1968, but *Batory* was temporarily retained for pleasure-cruising.

[333] *SOBIESKI* ('39) 1947–50 Swan Hunter
10,050t. 493 × 67 1–2 M–2 16k.

Built for a Polish South American service. After wartime trooping *Sobieski* was placed on the route, Naples–Genoa–Cannes–New York, and stayed there until sold to Russia, March 1950. She is now *Gruzia* and employed in the Black Sea.

STEFAN BATORY 1969– *See MAASDAM* [156

BALTIC STEAMSHIP COMPANY (1966–) *Russian*

FUNNEL – *White with broad red band bearing a yellow hammer-and-sickle*

FLAG – *Red; hammer-and-sickle and star, yellow*

HULL – *Black with white riband and green waterline*

The entire mercantile marine of the Union of Soviet Socialist Republics is state-owned and works under a common house-flag though administered by different 'companies' according to the area of operation. Shipping based on Baltic ports comes under the Baltic Steamship Company.

Russia, regardless of the ruling regime, has inevitably looked to Siberia to find new homes for her migrants and sources of raw materials. Consequently she has been a very late arrival on the North Atlantic. Westbound emigrants there certainly were from the Tsarist Empire, but they came almost exclusively from the politically dissatisfied western provinces and travelled in foreign ships—originally German and mainly British this century. The very poor Russian American Line of 1906 was basically Danish although under the Russian flag and ended with World War I.

On 14 April 1966 the Baltic Steamship Company's *Alexandr Pushkin* opened a new era, for on that day she cleared Leningrad on her maiden voyage to Montreal and has since sailed regularly to Canada during the months the St. Lawrence is ice-free. There are no winter sailings. Passage rates and accommodation standards correspond with those of other liners of similar size competing for the international transatlantic passenger traffic. Ports of call were originally Helsinki, Copenhagen, London and Quebec, but Copenhagen has now been dropped and Bremerhaven and Havre have been added.

[336] *ALEXANDR PUSHKIN* ('65) 1966– Wismar
19,850t. 509 × 77 1–1 M–2 20k.

Alexandr Pushkin (130 First, 620 Tourist) commissioned in August 1965 and was employed in the Black Sea for a short time. She takes her name from the greatest of Russian poets and is one of three German-built sisters which are Russia's largest liners other than *Sovetsky Sojus* (ex-German *Hansa* [191]).

EAST ASIATIC COMPANY (1946–1952) *Danish*

FLAG – *On white, a foul anchor set diagonally (crown to upper corner of hoist) and small letters 'Ø.K.' in lower corner—all in blue*

HULL – *Light grey with blue riband and green waterline*

Copenhagen is the Scandinavian port traditionally associated with overseas trading and Denmark almost inevitably anticipated Norwegian and Swedish entry into the New York trade under steam by many years. The Thingvalla Line, founded in 1880, met with little success and 18 years later was taken over by the United Steamship Company of Copenhagen who continued and improved the Thingvalla service under the new name, Scandinavian American Line. Rise of the Norwegian and Swedish transatlantic companies affected the Danish adversely and the World Depression caught the latter with an outdated fleet. The last ship (*Frederik VIII* of 1914, 11,850 tons) was laid up in 1935 and scrapped after two years. The Danes have since lacked a Western Ocean passenger line, but the confused conditions which followed termination of the 1939–45 War enabled the East Asiatic Company (Østasiatiske Kompagni) to find temporary employment for some passenger-freighters in the Copenhagen–New York trade.

The East Asiatic Company won a place in maritime history with *Selandia* of 1912, the first ocean-going motorship. She made no pretence of having a funnel, her exhaust gases being led away through an exhaust-pipe attached to the third mast, and the Danes were still adhering to this funnelless motorship profile in the 1940's. The Copenhagen–New York sailings commenced in March 1946 and were made direct. Allocation of a second vessel in 1949 allowed a sailing every third week for a time. Association with the Gdynia-America Line was close and withdrawal of *Batory* from the New York trade led to similar action by the East Asiatic early in 1951, although a ship temporarily revived the service the next year.

[341]	*JUTLANDIA* ('34)	1946–50	8450t.	425 × 61	0–4	M–2	15k.
[342]	*ERRIA* ('32)	1949–51	7650t.	439 × 62	0–4	M–2	15k.
[343]	*FALSTRIA* ('45	1952	7000t.	425 × 63	0–4	M–1	15k.

60, 74 and 54 First respectively. All built by Nakskov Works. *Jutlandia* left the Atlantic for conversion to a Korean War hospital ship.

APPENDIX

EARLY CHANGES IN THE CUNARD FUNNEL AND HOUSE-FLAG

The funnel and flags of the Cunard Steam-Ship Company's predecessor, the British & North American Royal Mail Steam Packet Company, have long been disputed, but no attempt seems ever to have been made to settle the issues. Adoption of a new funnel for the *Queen Elizabeth 2* brings these questions to the fore.

The funnel-change presents no real difficulty. Paintings of the pioneer Cunarders and also one of *Batavia* (1870) in private possession show a plain red funnel with black top. On the other hand many drawings of early Cunard ships show apparent black rings on the funnels, but these are certainly the shadows of funnel-irons. One such drawing is of *Gallia* (1879). After this date the lines on the funnels suddenly become firmer and thicker. This can only mean that the Cunard Steam-Ship Company added the black rings when they superseded the old company in 1879 and changed the house-flag. A particular reason for the addition existed. The old funnel had lost its distinction in 1864 when the Cie. Gle. Transatlantique steamers, also with black-topped red funnels, started berthing at New York.

The house-flag is more difficult. Two pennants (a blue with white saltire over a narrower red) are accepted as the original Cunard flag and were also used by Burns & MacIver's own vessels. At the other end of the scale an American publication of 1875 gives the flag as a blue burgee with large white star, and Inman and White Star booklets of 1878–9 confirm this. The same burgee appears in a coloured print of *Asia* (1850). Many drawings of the 1850's and 1860's show an obvious burgee and the author had seen none of a Cunarder flying the two pennants until recently. The belief the blue burgee was adopted about 1850 was, however, shattered when an *Illustrated London News* picture of *Russia* (1867) with the pennants came to light. *Illustrated London News* ship-drawings of the period are excellent in their detail and must be accepted an unimpeachable authority. What is the answer?

House-flags first came into use about 1820 and many early steamship companies had none. Pictures of the Cunard pioneers under the pennants are the exception rather than the rule. The highly decorative dinner plates supplied to the *Britannia*s depict each of the four steamships, but lack any sign of a house-flag. The blue burgee with star is known to have been the personal flag of Samuel Cunard. A reasonable deduction is that until after 1867 at earliest, the British & North American had no specific house-flag and each Cunarder flew the personal flag of the partner/partners holding the larger number of 64th-shares in her.

INDEX

INDEX

(Names in small type indicate ships which made only stray Transatlantic voyages and are merely mentioned in the text.)